Praise for *Challenging Words for Smart People*

"Richard Lederer's exuberant erudition is infectious as he unveils linguistic curiosities we take for granted and challenges us through quizzes to notice patterns and anomalies we've passed over. Lederer not only imposes order on chaos but also stretches readers' minds to recognize linguistic curiosities we take for granted. This book is as entertaining as it is educational, illustrating wordplay and then teasing readers with delightful quizzes."
　　—Rod L. Evans, author of *Tyrannosaurus Lex*

"When I picture Richard Lederer's mind, I see leprechauns with lexicons. Man, there's a lot going on in there."
　　—John Vorhaus, author of *Banana Pants Crazy*

"Come, all you word jugglers and letter-play lovers, the game is afoot! In *Challenging Words for Smart People*, Richard Lederer, America's punniest recreational linguist, invites you to match minds and wits with him in this effervescent collection of amusing essays and challenging quizzes. Lederer's brilliant and entertaining presentation of the oddities of our English vocabulary should appeal to anyone whose teeming brain is tickled by the weird and wonderful ways of words."
　　—Charles Harrington Elster, author of *Word Workout*, *Verbal Advantage*, and *What in the Word?*

"In *Challenging Words for Smart People*, Richard Lederer again demonstrates his astounding ability to ferret out every hidden treasure and sparkling gem that lurks in our endlessly fascinating English language. When it comes to being fecund, he isn't second! As a writer on language and wordplay myself, I'm in awe of his vast knowledge and inventive mind. This remarkable book teems with brain-teasing linguistic quizzes, puzzles, riddles, and games that you'll find entertaining and fun, even as you learn things you never knew before."
　　—Don Hauptman, author of *Cruel and Unusual Puns* and *Acronymania*

"It's a wonder that anyone learns to speak English. It's such a complicated language. Your reward for learning, though, is to be transported to the wonderful world of word and letter play. You couldn't have a better guide to that world than Richard Lederer in his book *Challenging Words for Smart People*. You'll have fun, and when you're done, you'll have seen aspects of English you never thought about before. Get ready to hang on to your hat. We're not in Kansas anymore."

—**Caroline McCullagh**, coauthor of *American Trivia*

Praise for Richard Lederer

"Columnist and punster Richard Lederer may be William Safire's only living peer at writing about grammar, word usage, and derivations."

—*Washington Post Book World*

"Lederer beguiles and bedazzles."

—*Los Angeles Times*

"Richard Lederer is the true King of Language Comedy."

—**Sidney Sheldon**, author of *After the Darkness*

"Columnist Extraordinaire."

—*The New Yorker*

"Richard Lederer opens the treasure chest of English and delights in each shiny coin he finds."

—**Rob Kyff**, a.k.a. "The Word Guy," nationally syndicated-language columnist and author of *Once Upon a Word*

"Richard Lederer's delight in English is itself delightful and contagious!"

—**Edwin Newman**, author of *Strictly Speaking* and *A Civil Tongue*

"Richard Lederer ought to be declared a national treasure."

—*Richmond Times-Dispatch*

CHALLENGING WORDS
for
SMART
PEOPLE

Also by Richard Lederer

Adventures of a Verbivore
Amazing Words
American Trivia (with Caroline McCullagh)
American Trivia Quiz Book (with Caroline McCullagh)
Anguished English
Animal Cracker Uppers Junior (with Jim Ertner)
The Ants Are My Friends (with Stan Kegel)
Basic Verbal Skills (with Philip Burnham)
The Big Book of Word Play Crosswords (with Gayle Dean)
The Bride of Anguished English
Building Bridge (with Bo Schambelan and Arnold Fisher)
The Circus of Words
Classic Literary Trivia
Cleverly Comical Animal Jokes (with Jim Ertner)
Comma Sense (with John Shore)
Crazy English
The Cunning Linguist
Fractured English
Get Thee to a Punnery
The Giant Book of Animal Jokes (with Jim Ertner)
The Gift of Age
Have Yourself a Punny Little Christmas
Hilarious Holiday Humor (with Stan Kegel)
Lederer on Language
Literary Trivia
A Man of My Words
The Miracle of Language
Monsters Unchained!
More Anguished English
The Play of Words
Presidential Trivia
Pun & Games
Puns Spooken Here
The Revenge of Anguished English
Rip Roaring Animal Jokes (with Jim Ertner)
Sleeping Dogs Don't Lay (with Richard Dowis)
Super Funny Animal Jokes (with Jim Ertner)
A Treasury for Cat Lovers
A Treasury for Dog Lovers
A Tribute to Teachers
Wild & Wacky Animal Jokes (with Jim Ertner)
The Word Circus
Word Wizard
The Write Way (with Richard Dowis)

CHALLENGING WORDS

for

SMART

PEOPLE

BRINGING ORDER TO THE ENGLISH LANGUAGE

RICHARD LEDERER

Marion Street Press
Portland, Oregon

To American Mensa,
with gratitude for the many friends I've made
and the good times I've had

Acknowledgments

Bob McKenty and Al Gregory contributed examples to "A Foul Ghoul Soul Loves Good Blood Food" and Norm Storer to "Fortunate Reversals." Dave Morice co-wrote "The Holy Grail of Letter Play." Kern Mann helped form the idea for "Highly Irregular Verbs." Some chapters in this book appeared in an earlier form in *The Word Circus* (Merriam-Webster 1998), *Crazy English* (Pocket Books 1989), and *Word Ways: The Journal of Recreational Linguistics*.

Published by Marion Street Press
4207 SE Woodstock Blvd # 168
Portland, OR 97206-6267
USA
http://www.marionstreetpress.com/

Orders and review copies: (800) 888-4741

Printed in the United States of America
ISBN 9781936863693

Back cover photo by Hoffman Photographic

Library of Congress Cataloging-in-Publication Data pending

CONTENTS

ON-WORD AND UP-WORD!

L anguage is like the air we breathe: It's invisible. It's all around us. We can't get along without it. Yet we take it for granted. But when we step back and listen to the sounds that escape from the holes in people's faces and examine the words that luminesce up on our screens, we are in for a lifetime of joy.

This book is not for everyone. But if you, like me, are heels-over-head nuts about language and have a passion for snatching significance from the mass of data swirling around us, you will share herein some sublime adventures in re-creation-al linguistics.

Like Julius Caesar's Gaul, *Challenging Words* is divided into three parts. The first part, "Sight, Sound, and Sense," plumbs the relationship between how English words are written and how those letters sound. The second part, "Letter-Perfect Challenges," calls up the collide-o-scopic alphabet to dance before our bedazzled eyes. The third part explores "The Glamour of Grammar." Reading that cluster, you may have more fun with grammar than ever before.

Each chapter states a challenge or two. In each READER CHALLENGE you'll have a chance to apply your bulked-up linguistic skills by drinking in data and playing word games. Your axons, dendrites, ganglia, and synapses will get quite a workout as you engage in a series of push-ups of the mind and aerobics of the brain.

Be prepared for a caboodle of lists and charts. I've painstakingly compiled them not to put you to sleep but to wake you up to the ability of the human mind to organize the rough and tumble of our speaking and the tough and rumble of our writing. My mission is to impose order on chaos and to sprinkle fairy dust on the familiar and mundane. It's your decision whether to poke around each miniature museum of words and occasionally stop to browse an exhibit or to contemplate each display and glimpse the abundant harvest of our bountiful, multifoliate language.

I have been computer-aided in writing several chapters, but most of the wordwork in this book is not susceptible to what computers do, only to what the computer we call the human brain is capable of doing. It's my word-happy, wordstruck, wordaholic, word-bethumped mind mining the whirled world for linguistic gold and pounding that precious metal into glowing artifacts for your entertainment and edification. I prefer artifice intelligence to artificial intelligence.

Again I caution you that this book is not for everyone. Its title reflects my firm belief in Truth in Labeling. If you've read this far and you love learning dressed up to have fun, you may be just the smart person this book is made for.

Richard Lederer
www.verbivore.com
richardhlederer@gmail.com

SIGHT, SOUND,
AND SENSE

ONCE UPON A
RHYME TIME

THE CHALLENGE:

How many natural rhymes can be
crammed into a single narrative?

We usually think of rhyme as a musical device found only in poems. But in fact, rhyme is the name of the game. Rhyme appeals so powerfully to the human ear that, if we listen carefully, we can discover a surprising number of common, everyday words and phrases that contain rhyme. Let's sneak a peek at the saga of Chicken Licken:

Once upon a rhyme time, Chicken Licken got the heebie-jeebies that the sky was falling. Figuring that with one's mojo it's use it or lose it, Licken dashed pell-mell, helter-skelter, hither and thither, higgledy-piggledy, hugger-mugger, willy nilly, balls-to-the-wall, and here, there, and everywhere, shouting, "Yoo hoo! May Day! You snooze, you lose! This isn't sci-fi! It's the real deal for double trouble! Birds of a feather, flock together! The sky is falling!"

Keeping his eyes on the prize, Chicken Licken came upon Henny Penny, a roly-poly, jelly-bellied old hen no longer in her heyday. Henny Penny huffed and puffed at Licken, "Tee-hee, I don't want to create ill will with a blame game, but what's all this hubbub and hurly burly about? Your whale of a tale sounds like a lot of phony baloney, folderol, razzmatazz, claptrap, and mumbo jumbo to me. I'm not a hick from the sticks. I don't believe in abracadabra and hocus-pocus voodoo, and I don't want to kowtow to a shock jock with a hodgepodge of pie in the sky."

"Jeepers creepers and geez Louise! That's a low blow with a blackjack," clucked Licken, who was left high and dry with his spirit at half staff. "It's not easy-peasy trying to do my fair share by being fair and square to all those near and dear to me. Why are you making such a to-do and taking potshots and calling my story a rinky-dinky hunk of junk? Hey, a friend in need is a friend indeed. I'm no Humpty-Dumpty crumbum. I may cry 'boohoo,' but I'm not a rumdum hobo panhandling with a squeegee for freebees and out to commit hari-kari. Sticks and stones may break my bones, but your opinion will never make or break me."

Backtracking, Chicken Licken went off looking for Cocky Locky to tell him that the sky was falling. But Locky was too busy being a large-and-in-charge, crackerjack hotshot and a hoity-toity wheeler dealer out and about downtown to wine and dine bigwigs, throwing funny money at jet-set fat cats with big paydays, and hobnobbing with dressed-for-success rich bitches at fancy-schmantzy wingdings.

Feeling the wear and tear and lumps and bumps of walking a fine line through a stress test, off Licken scurried to hippy-dippy Loosey Goosey, who was indeed loose as a goose and snug as a bug in a rug. "Whadaya know, daddy-o?" honked Goosey. "Hey, you old son of a gun. Don't be a namby pamby boy toy. Let's take a chill pill, go with the flow, and party hearty. I've got a razzle-dazzle, killer-diller, chockablock, no-fuss-no-muss idea that's the bee's knees and will float your boat, flick your Bic, and knock your block, jock, and socks off. Let's get down to the nitty-gritty and hustle our bustle to a spring fling attended by artsy-fartsy Deadheads who meet and greet, have tons of fun in the sun, and feel their flower power while smoking mellow yellow wacky tobacky. With the fans wearing their backpacks, tie-dyed shirts, and zoot suits, it'll be a real blast from the past like a stun gun.

"It'll be better than prime time on the boob tube or a chick flick at a picnic on a bedspread—a sure cure for all your gloom and doom. We'll get palsy-walsy with hotsy-totsy tootsie-wootsies who get sky-high ready to do handstands on the grandstands and the bandstand and then do the hootchy-kootchy, boogie-woogie, hokey pokey, and funky monkey with redheads as they get hot to trot and ready to make hanky-panky.

"Be there or be square! We'll be made in the shade and in like Flynn with all those lovey-dovey cutesy-wootsies, which I promise we'll share even Stephen. If you want to be a fuddy duddy no-show, then I'll see you later, alligator."

"After a while, crocodile, but not while the sky is falling," replied Licken, and he put the pedal to the metal and went to waylay his friend herky-jerky Turkey Lurkey. But plug-ugly Lurkey wasn't any help either. In fact, he was more harum-scarum and flibberty gibberty than Licken, acting like a Silly Billy bozo, a run-and-gun local yokel hillbilly pogo sticking around like a lamebrain locofoco who was drunk as a skunk with a peg leg. "What can one teeny-weeny, itsy bitsy piece of sky falling down matter?" gobbled Lurkey like a ding-a-ling kiwi, eager beaver, and funny bunny trying to play a solo on an oboe, a piccolo, and a hurdy gurdy at the same time.

Feeling like a Hottentot with ants in his pants, Chicken Licken decided that his court of last resort was to get back on track by consulting fuzzy-wuzzy Foxy Loxy. Licken was sick of the humdrum, ragtag hoi polloi and their honky-tonk ways, while Loxy's claim to fame was that he was a true blue guru.

"Okeydokey, you lucky duck," said Loxy with a tutti-fruity smile. "Your goof-proof, rough-and-tough, rock'em sock'em story takes the cake and fills the bill by hook and by crook, lock, stock, and barrel. Yo, bro. Let's go to my teepee for a powwow and a chalktalk." So off the two ran to Loxy's den, where Loxy began to speed-read his handy-dandy cookbook about slicing and dicing sweetmeat and Tex Mex green beans and chugalugging them down with mai tais, Tia Marias, pale ale, and near beer.

At this, Chicken Licken sensed double trouble and yelled, "Ah ha! Oh ho! Who says that might makes right? I'm not a meals on wheels, you big pig and beast from the east! Never ever! Now it's a no go! We're one and done!"

"Holy moley and hell's bells, peewee. Loose lips sink ships. You're cruisin' for a bruisin', your ass is grass, and you are screwed, blued, and tattooed. No pain; no gain. That seals the deal. It's my way or the highway," snarled Loxy, looking less and less like a Care Bear and more and more like a lean, mean eating machine singing, "Winner! Winner! Chicken dinner!"

"No way, Jose, and up your nose with a rubber hose," shot back Licken, as he beat a retreat. "Don't be a nitwit in a shit fit! This cave could really use a sump pump and a pooper scooper, you unsanitary bowwow. I'm off to Fiji, Hong Kong, Togo, Malay, Tora Bora, or Zululand—anyplace but here!"

Then wham, bam, thank you, ma'am. The sky fell down and killed them all, proving that haste makes waste, well begun is only half done, and a stitch in time may not save nine.

A FOUL GHOUL
SOUL LOVES
GOOD BLOOD FOOD

THE CHALLENGE:

What are the largest clusters
of words that look as if
they rhyme, but don't?

L ong, long ago, in 1833 to be exact, one Thomas Haynes Bayly
wrote the song "Long, Long Ago." Here is the first and best-
known verse:

Tell me the tales that to me were so dear,
Long, long ago, long, long ago.
Sing me the songs I delighted to hear,
Long, long ago, long ago.
Now you are come, all my grief is removed.
Let me forget that so long you have roved.
Let me believe that you love as you loved,
Long, long ago, long ago.

In the fifth through seventh lines of his poem, Bayly dreamt up a path-breaking eye rhyme—*removed, roved,* and *loved*—three words with the same last letters, *-oved,* but three different soundings.

Eye rhymes (or sight rhymes) are words that look like rhymes but don't sound like rhymes. The conceit here is that the viewer of these eye-dentities must focus on the replication of letters that appear in the final syllable or syllables in each of two or more words and ignore the actual sound of those letters and the placement of stress.

Eye rhymes provide dramatic testimony to the phoneme-grapheme chasm that stretches across our glorious, notorious, uproarious, outrageous, courageous, contagious, stupendous, tremendous, end-over-endous English language. The most cheerfully democratic and hospitable language in history, English has welcomed into its vocabulary words ancient and modern, far and near, including their divergent spellings. In *The Devil's Dictionary,* Ambrose Bierce defines *orthography* as "the science of spelling by the eye instead of the ear. Advocated with more heat than light by the outmates of every asylum for the insane." Edward Rondthaler, the inventor of the Soundspel System, labels spelling "a sort of graphic stutter we've tolerated for generations." "Spelling," declares Mario Pei, "is the world's most awesome mess."

Much of that mess has accumulated from the fact that one set of letters can represent a number of sounds. That's why a foreign student when asked what word the letters *m-a-n-s-l-a-u-g-h-t-e-r* spelled, responded, "man's laughter." That's why, it is said, *anger* is just one letter away from *danger.* That's why a star university lineman who was told he could play football if he could get just a single letter right in the spelling of *coffee,* responded, "k-a-u-p-h-y," not a correct letter in the batch!

The pairing of *anger* and *danger* demonstrates the possibility of semantic kinship between eye rhymes—*evil-devil, damp-swamp, ponder-wonder, height-weight, hover-over, alliance-dalliance, primal-animal,* and *power-mower*—and opposites—*here-there, your-our, friend-fiend, treat-threat,* and *pleasant-malfeasant.*

The intrepid hunter-gatherer of words and letters experiences an adrenaline rush when such a promising category of words cavorts into view, but capturing double-eye rhymes presents little challenge. As you'll see in the upcoming "Eye Rhymes" game, examples of seeing double are a dime a dozen—and there are dozens of dozens. Still, I can't resist showing off my favorite pairs for their elegance and surprise: *simply-imply, patio-ratio, hoist-soloist, priest-funniest, unit-whodunit, stately-philately, scavenger-avenger, radios-adios, guest-bluest, salty-realty, myopic-biopic, tenacity-intracity, younger-scrounger, Buick-quick, overage-coverage, Buick-quick,* and *Vaseline-baseline.*

Let's move directly to triple plays, quadruple plays, and even more pyrotechnic plays that consist of familiar words. But before the parade of lists, let's establish the criteria for what constitutes genuine, authentic, certified eye rhymes:

In each cluster, the eye-rhymed vowel and all succeeding letters must be identical, but, in each example, the consonant that comes right before that vowel must be different. Thus, the likes of *story-history, rice-licorice, limb-climb, liar-familiar,* and *science-conscience-prescience* do not qualify as eye rhymes. The single exception to this rule is if a word, such as *pace, Maria, Quixote,* and *lough,* sparks forth two different soundings. In these instances, I count both.

Barred also are rhymes that depend on absorbed anterior vowels, such as in *cat-swat-heat, pint-mint-taint,* and *on-won-moon.* Independent anterior vowels, those that do not directly affect the eye-rhymed vowels, are allowed, as in *on-won-neon, beat-caveat-whereat,* and *vein - stein-wherein.*

Contractions are forbidden, such as *front-font-don't* and *led-diced-we'd.*

On the other hand, words are allowed in which the accent does not fall on the "rhyming" syllables, as in *racy-legacy, icy-policy,* and *acre-massacre.* Such examples are permitted because the convention for eye rhymes is that the viewer pretends to be deaf and focuses only on the identity of the crucial vowel(s) and all succeeding letters.

Now feast your eyes on two hundred triple and quadruple constellations and beyond. It's your decision whether to sip or binge, hurry or tarry, browse or carouse.

TRIPLE EYE RHYMES

foul-ghoul-soul	good-blood-food
love-move-rove	oven-cloven-proven
star-war-beggar	tasty-angioplasty-dynasty
page-postage-mirage	card-ward-standard
sassy-classy-embassy	friar-caviar-familiar
band-wand-errand	zeroed-canoed-coed
poster-roster-foster	fruit-circuit-intuit
pager-lager-dowager	prior-superior-senior
date-climate-karate	hot-parrot-depot
pass-bass (ace)-cutlass	heater-sweater-theater
maid-said-plaid	come-home-epitome
fear-bear-linear	early-dearly-linearly
anted-wanted-panted	china-patina-stamina
wallet-mallet-ballet	get-closet-ballet
fruity-gratuity-equity	time-regime-anime
wiped-gossiped-biped	duped-larruped-quadruped
dial-serial-facial	eon-nickelodeon-pigeon
father-gather-bather	salve-valve-halve
prison-bison-unison	going-doing-boing
diner-mariner-pristiner	copy-dopy-canopy
bravado-tornado-ado	oblige-vestige-prestige
somber-bomber-beachcomber	longed-gonged-sponged
mature-nature-stature	hive-give-naive
heist-atheist-ageist	doused-roused-rendezvoused

gala-koala-impala

wily-lily-family

preyed-keyed-eyed

volcano-piano-guano

native-combative-negative

bad-wad-salad

science-experience-patience

cheder-interceder-seder

are-bare-curare (*ah-ree*)

dent-latent-denouement (*ah*)

wait-parfait-portrait (*uht*)

staged-camouflaged-aged (*ayj-ed*)

waver-cadaver-aver

rhino-casino-domino

sonata-strata-data (*ayt-uh*)

eases-ceases-pancreases

ringed-hinged-winged (*ing-id*)

doggy-foggy-loggy (*oh-gee*)

discrete-fete (*ate*)-naivete (*tay*)

sorry-worry-lorry (*aw-ree*)

gross-loss-albatross (*ahss*)

dual-ritual-menstrual (*al*)

amber-chamber-clamber (*ammer*)

call-shall-pall-mall (*pell-mell*)

pays-says-cays (*eez*)

chance-nuance-distance

writer-liter-arbiter

irate-pirate-emirate

ago-lumbago-virago

diva-saliva-gingiva

lousy-mousy-jealousy

client-ingredient-transient

omen-women-abdomen (*uh-min*)

talked-faxed-wasted

pain-again-certain

toes-shoes-does (*uhz*)

used-bused (*ust*)-focused (*ist*)

very-query-machinery (*ih-ree*)

niche-quiche-cliché

word-chord-record (*urd*)

fade-facade (*ahd*)-forbade (*ad*)

most-lost-accost (*ahst*)

sort-rapport (*ore*)-effort (*ert*)

zany-many-company (*ih-nee*)

cart-wart-braggart (*ert*)

anal-canal-banal (*uh-nahl*)

body-melody-polypody (*oh-dee*)

pony-agony-irony (*er-nee*)

table-lovable-liable (*eye-bull*)

front-font-wont (*ohnt*)

pass-bass (*ace*)-cutlass

fester-rhymester-Gloucester

foe-canoe-Zoe (*oh-ee*)

lemon-demon-Pokemon

began-vegan-Megan

cod-period-Pernod

halo-buffalo-Palo Alto

ride-bona fide-Candide

gavel-navel-Ravel

boat-waistcoat (*it*)-Croat (*oh-at*)

pipe-recipe-Filipe

vague-ague-Prague

hope-calliope-Europe

daze-kamikaze-Lamaze

fussy-pussy-Debussy

sciatica-pica-Costa Rica

zebra-algebra-Debra

doer-playgoer-Boer

taco-Waco-Monaco

sequin-ruin-Gauguin (*an*)

QUADRUPLE EYE RHYMES
(This may be the place to start taking a closer look.)

cut-put-debut-gamut

vein-protein-stein-wherein

hour-four-your-glamour

pale-locale-finale-tamale

bus-fetus-menus-au jus

cayuses-buses-focuses-muses

later-water-alma mater-theater

grosses-losses-albatrosses (*ah-sez*) -posses

touch-pouch-scaramouch (*oosh, ootch*)

shoved-moved-roved-beloved (*uh-vedd*)

prom-whom-shalom-atom

pal-wherewithal-banal-medical

bared-collared-radared-infrared

ion (*eye-ahn*)–lion (*eye-in*)-champion-nation

ally-dally-mentally-wally

loner-goner-prisoner-couponer

competes-fetes (*ates*)-diabetes-machetes

deceit-counterfeit-gesundheit-albeit

famous-bayous-rendezvous-miaous-(ouze)

case-phrase-vase (*ahz*)-blase (*ah-zay*)

role-hyperbole (*uh-lee*)-guacamole (*oh-lee*)-posole (*oh-lay*)

swan-pan-sultan (*in*)-orangutan (*ang*)

prior-superior-junior (*yer*)-seignior (*yor*)

die-menagerie-lingerie (*ay*)-prima facic (*uh*)

comb-bomb-tomb-aplomb (*uhm*)

fund-fecund (*ihnd*)-bund (*oohnd*)-dachshund (*oohnt*)

change-flange-mélange-orange (*indge*)

fallow-swallow-allow-marshmallow (*ell-oh*)

there-were-mere-consigliere (*air-ee*)

name-sesame-macrame (*uh-may*)-grand dame (*ahm*)

path-swath-math-Sabbath

bite-elite-granite-Yosemite

douse-arouse-youse-Toulouse

larceny-deny-Allegheny-Matheny

debutante-vigilante-andante-Plante

armada-cicada-Nevada-Canada

bus-focus-au jus (*oo*)-Belarus (*oose*)

dual (*ool*)-usual-equal-victual (*it'l*)-Pasqual

tape-agape (*uh-pay*)-serape (*ah-pee*)-Lenape (uh-pee)

bead-head-Gilead-Sinead (*ayd*)

aria-malaria-Maria (*ee-uh* and *eye-uh*)

south-youth-mouth (*outhe*, as a verb)-Portsmouth (*ith*)

armada-cicada-Nevada-Canada

QUINTUPLE EYE RHYMES

beat-great-sweat-caveat-whereat

his-tennis-alibis-debris-hadjis

these-obese-diocese (uhs)-marchese *(ay-zuh)*-Genovese *(ee-zee)*

ache-mustache-panache *(ahsh)*-attaché-Apache

vary-salary-aviary-calamary *(ah-ree)*-elementary *(tree)*

pat-swat-what-carat-baccarat *(ah)*

pant-restaurant-want *(uhnt)*-infant *(int)*-croissant *(ah)*

sea-yea *(ay)*-idea-azalea *(yuh)*-mea *(ay-uh,* as in *mea culpa)*

cloth-both-mammoth-doth-betroth *(ohthe)*

bias-alias-cafeterias-dementias-strias *(eye-uhz)*

yes-crises-foxes-makes-dabbles

competed-ticketed-feted (ayt-ed)-parqueted-macheted

extol-alcohol-petrol *(uhl)*-pol *(ahl)*-sol *(oh,* as in the music scale)

aches-caches-mustaches-detaches-spinaches

bone-done-gone-abalone *(oh-nee)*-anemone *(uh-nee)*

ices-polices-offices-licorices-indices *(ih-ceez)*

precise-promise-rise-valise *(eece)*-expertise *(eez)*

promises-rises-paradises-valises-crises *(eye-seez)*

cases-oases *(ay-seez)*-gases-phases *(ayzes)*-vases *(ahziz)*

roses-doses-loses-purposes-psychoses *(eez)*

rose-dose-lose-purpose-Jose

bean-ocean-protean *(ee-in)*-Sean *(awn)*-Chilean *(ay-en)*

changes-flanges-mélanges-oranges-Ganges

tiara-baccara-mascara *(eh-ruh)*-Sara-Niagara

dates-climates-pilates *(ah-teez)*-Socrates *(uh-teez)* Euphrates *(ay-teez)* dote-coyote-garrote *(aht)*-Quixote *(oh-tay, it)*

SEXTUPLE EYE RHYMES

tier-flier-carrier-dossier-soldier-chevalier (*yay*)

pat-swat-what-carat-baccarat (*ah*)- éclat (*ay*)

cave-have-suave-octave (ive)-agave (*ah-vee*)-grave (*ah-vay*)

memos-adios-chaos-cosmos (*us*)-apropos-dos (*ooz*, as in *dos and don'ts*)

pine-marine-engine-aborigine-(*ihn-ee*), linguine (*ee-nee*)-sine (*ihn-ih*, as in *sine qua non*)

brioche (*ohsh, ahsh*)-caroche (*ohch, ahsh*), synecdoche (*uh-kee*)-troche (*oh-kee*)

lace-menace-demi-glace (*ahs, ah-say*)-pace (*ah-chay*)-Liberace

file-automobile-facile (*uhl*)-simile-campanile (*ee-lee*)-Chile (*ee-lay*)

noise-porpoise-vichyssoise-bourgeoise (*whaz*)-Eloise-Boise

SEPTUPLE EYE RHYMES

ton-on-don-common (*in*)-iron (*ern*)-chaperon (*ohn*)-bon (*oh*, as in *bon mot*)

seas-yeas (*ays*)-ideas-pancreas-whereas-hydrangeas (*uhs*) San Andreas

dice-police-office-licorice (*ish*)-vice (*eye-suh*, as in *vice versa*)-Nice-Eurydice (*ih-che*)

NONUPLE EYE RHYME

was-has-gas-spas (*ahz*)-canvas (*iss*)-dogmas (*ihz*)-gravitas (*ahss*)-mardi gras (*ah*)-Arkansas (*aw*)

AND THE CHAMPION?

(twelve soundings, but some with the same lead-off consonant):

bough-dough-enough-cough-hiccough-lough   (*ock,   och*)-through-trough (*awth*)-thorough (*uh*)-Hough (*ahf*)-Colclough (*ee*).

Here's a sentence that contains all the pronunciations of the letter combination –*ough*:

Coughing and hiccoughing, a thoughtful, thorough, rough, doughboy ploughman named Colclough Hough waded through a lough to reach his trough.

EYE RHYMES

READER CHALLENGE:

Stop, look, and listen. Examine the fifty words below and think of a second word that is an eye rhyme, that is, a word that looks like a rhyme but isn't. The answers are all one syllable, as in *honored-bored* and *eunuch-much*.

1. leaf 2. foot 3. beard 4. wolf 5. owl 6. mint 7. pooch 8. feast 9. earth 10. goof

11. hook 12. own 13. fool 14. clasp 15. dog 16. geese 17. cash 18. keen 19. peak 20. quite

21. blew 22. patch 23. rouge 24. wharf 25. death 26. goose 27. roll 28. mouse 29. paste 30. work

31. friend 32. bought 33. toad 34. valve 35. soup 36. raft 37. harm 38. taunt 39. full 40. cow

41. worth 42. grieve 43. push 44. huge 45. niche 46. cease 47. matinee 48. concierge 49. shitake 50. antipodes

Now, and with a greater degree of difficulty, the answers to the next hundred posers are all polysyllabic, as in *only-wantonly* and *triad-myriad*.

51. strict 52. opus 53. cue 54. these 55. bond 56. see 57. rule 58. babble 59. courage 60. final

61. joke 62. cable 63. spiny 64. never 65. oval 66. bee 67. passage, 68. coin 69. prayer 70. despite

71. total 72. serpentine 73. dozen 74. denial 75. discount 76. jury 77. marry 78. steady 79. bully 80. lowly

81. finger 82. into 83. picked 84. folder 85. model 86. latent 87. valor 88. laughter 89. binder 90. mother

91. whallop 92. preface 93. lumber 94. even 95. duet 96. ether 97. budding 98. stringy 99. saddle 100. battle

101. feather 102. potato 103. aria 104. gander 105. hunger 106. daughter 107. pollen 108. garden 109. kilo 110. timber

111. riot 112. armada 113. delicate 114. honor 115. axis 116. tasted 117. fetal 118. decal 119. cited 120. mistress

121. marble 122. pretty 123. elude 124. journey 125. solo 126. forest 127. allied 128. starchy 129. tremble 130. choir

131. drama 132. rely 133. oral 134. wider 135. gamy 136. postage 137.anemic 138. caret 139. holy 140. gory

141. sadist 142. magna 143. gorilla 144. saga 145. bible 146. status 147. homer 148. deity 149. shovel 150. elevator

Answers

1. deaf 2. boot 3. heard 4. golf 5. bowl 6. pint 7. brooch 8. breast 9. hearth 10. hoof

11. spook 12. down 13. wool 14. wasp 15. hog 16. cheese 17. wash 18. been 19. break 20. suite

21. sew 22. watch 23. gouge 24. scarf 25. heath 26. choose 27. doll 28. rouse 29. caste 30. cork

31. fiend 32. drought 33. broad 34. salve 35. coup 36. waft 37. warm 38. aunt 39. dull 40. tow

41. north 42. sieve 43. rush 44. luge 45. quiche 46. please 47. bee 48. merge 49. cake 50. codes

51. indict 52. octopus 53. segue 54. obese 55. second 56. puree 57. schedule 58. squabble 59. entourage 60. medicinal

61. karaoke 62. syllable 63. destiny 64. fever 65. removal 66. matinee 67. massage 68. heroin 69. layer 70. respite

71. pivotal 72. turpentine 73. frozen 74. menial 75. viscount 76. bury 77. quarry 78. beady 79. gully 80. jowly

81. ginger 82. pinto 83. wicked 84. solder 85. yodel 86. patent 87. squalor 88. daughter 89. tinder 90. bother

91. whallop 92. deface 93. dumber 94. seven 95. suet 96. tether 97. pudding 98. stingy 99. waddle 100. wattle

101. breather 102. gelato 103. malaria 104. wander 105. plunger 106. laughter 107. swollen 108. warden 109. silo 110. climber

111. idiot 112. cicada 113. masticate 114. donor 115. taxis 116. lasted 117. petal 118. fecal 119. exited 120. distress

121. warble 122. petty 123. prelude 124. tourney 125. piccolo 126. sorest 127. rallied 128. monarchy 129. ensemble 130. reservoir

131. panorama 132. completely 133. pastoral 134. consider 135. infamy 136. hostage 137. academic 138. cabaret 139. monopoly 140. history

141. jihadist 142. lasagna 143. tortilla 144. rutabaga 145. terrible 146. hiatus 147. customer 148. spontaneity 149. grovel 150. senator

ORTHOGRAPHE
MIRABILE

THE CHALLENGE:

What sound in English can be
represented by the greatest variety
of letters or letter combinations?

With the possible exceptions of presidents, sports commis-
sioners, and taxes, there exists no more popular object of
abuse and ridicule than our "system" of English spelling.
"It is wildly erratic and almost wholly without logic," contends J.
Donald Adams. "One needs the eye of a hawk, the ear of a dog, and
the memory of an elephant to make headway against its confusions
and inconsistencies."

These are strong words, but even the briefest glance at the situation reveals that the accusations are just. In what other language could one find the pairs *moveable* and *immovable, harass* and *embarrass,* and *deceit* and *receipt?*

The main cause of all the whoop-de-do (also whoop-de-doo) about English orthography is the whopping distance between the sounds of our words and their spelling. This state of affairs is created by the inadequacy of the Roman alphabet to represent the sounds of English; our cheerful willingness to borrow words and, with them, unconventional spellings, from more than three hundred other languages; and, finally, changes in our pronunciation, most of which have not been matched by changes in our orthography. The result is that about eighty percent of our words are not spelled phonetically; in effect, we have two languages, one spoken and one written.

Now let us reverse our field. Not only can certain letters represent a number of different sounds, but we find that a single sound can be represented by many different letters. George Bernard Shaw, who bequeathed a sizable (also sizeable) sum of money to the cause of simplified spelling, announced that he had discovered a new way to spell the word *fish.* His fabrication turned out to be *ghoti: gh* as in rou*gh, o* as in w*o*men, and *ti* as in na*ti*on. There are many other "fish" in the A-B-Seas, including these ten:

phusi: ph as in <u>ph</u>ysic, *u* as in b<u>u</u>sy, *si* as in pen<u>si</u>on;
pheat: gra<u>phe</u>d, embarra<u>ss</u>, ini<u>ti</u>ate;
ffess: o<u>ff</u>, pr<u>e</u>tty, i<u>ss</u>ue;
ughyce: la<u>ugh</u>, h<u>y</u>mn, o<u>ce</u>an;
ugheiossi: ro<u>ughe</u>d, port<u>io</u>n, mi<u>ss</u>ion;
Pfeechsi: <u>Pf</u>eiffer, b<u>ee</u>n, fu<u>chs</u>ia;
pphiapsh: sa<u>pph</u>ire, marr<u>ia</u>ge, <u>psh</u>aw;
fuiseo: <u>f</u>at, g<u>ui</u>lt, naus<u>eou</u>s;
ftaisch: so<u>ft</u>en, vill<u>ai</u>n, <u>sch</u>wa;
ueiscio: lie<u>u</u>tenant (British pronunciation), forf<u>ei</u>t, con<u>sci</u>ous.

In the previous chapter of this book, I explored the limits of end-rhymes. Now, rather than restricting the search to letter combinations at the end of words, I ask: What sound can be represented by the greatest variety of letters or letter combinations in English spelling? In chasing the answer to this White Whale of a question, I had to make a crucial decision:

Since sound and spelling don't match in English, how does one know how to allocate which printed letters to which sounds? In particular, if a silent consonant follows or precedes a vowel or combination of vowels, as in *aisle, feign, rhebok,* and *ginkgo,* should that consonant be credited to the variant spelling of that vowel sound? As sole arbiter, I have decided that it should. In other words, if a certain sound springs from the territory inhabited by a cluster of letters, all those letters are assigned responsibility for generating that sound.

Here, then, are my chief lowercase and uppercase candidates for orthographic heterogeneity. For convenience, I list the cluster spellings alphabetically:

SH (27 variants):

C appreciate	PSH pshaw	SCIO conscious	SS assure
CE ocean	S sugar	SEO nauseous	SSH Asshu
CH chef	SC crescendo	SH shoe	SSHE Bysshe
CHE quiche	SCH schwa	SHCH shchio	SSI mission
CHSI fuchsia	SCHE tusche	SHE wished	SZ szlachta
CI suspicion	SCHSCH	SI mansion	T initiate
HS Hsian	eschscholzia	SJ sjömil	TI nation

EYE (36 variants):

A naive	AIY Rubaiyat	HI rhino	IJ rijsttafel
AAI braai	AU Dolgallau	HY why	IS island
AE maestro	AY Haydn	I I	IVE fivepence
AEI scarabaei	AYE aye	IC indict	O coyote
AI samurai	EI heist	IE tie	UI guidance
AIE shanghaied	EIGH height	IG sign	UY buy
AILLE trouvaille	EY geyser	IGH high	UYE guyed
AILLES Versailles	EYE eye	IGHE sighed	Y my
AIS aisle	HAI kowhai	IGHY Nighy	YE rye

OH (52 variants):

AO Curacao	EOT Peugeot	OA oak	OO brooch
AOH pharaoh	EOU Seoul	OAH American Pharoah	OP de trop
AU chauvinist	EUX Clarenceux	OAT boatswain	OS apropos
AUD Rimbaud	EW sew	OD Pernod	OST Prevost
AULD La Rochefoucauld	EWE sewed	OE toe	OT depot
AULT Foucault	GO ginkgo	OEH Poehler	OTE picoted
AULX Prevaulx	HAU haute couture	OEW Loew	OTHE clothes
AUT comme il faut	HAUD Milhaud	OEWE Loewe	OTS bon mots
AUX faux	HAUT haut monde	OG cologne	OU soul
EAU bureau	HO ghost	OGH Van Gogh	OUGH dough
EAUX trousseaux	HOA whoa	OH oh	OUGHE furloughed
EAUE plateaued	HOE echoed	OHE ohed	OW tow
EO yeoman	O go	OL yolk	OWE owe

This list has inspired me to become such a Wizard of OHs that I now unveil a twenty-three word sentence in which every word yields an OH sound, yet each OH is spelled differently:

Although Seoul yeoman folk owe Pharaoh's Vaud bureau hoed oats, gauche Van Gogh, swallowing Curacao cognac oh so soulfully, sews grosgrain, pictoted, brooched chapeaux.

OO (52 variants):

AULT Sault	IEWE viewed	OUGHA brougham	UEUE queue
EAU beauty	IOUX Sioux	OUGHE sloughed	UGH Hugh
EU sleuth	IU jiu-jitsu	OUI bouillon	UGHE Hughes
EUX Devereux	O to	OUP coup	UH buhl
EW brew	OE canoe	OUPE couped	UI suit
EWE chewed	OEU manoeuvre	OUR bourgeois	US au jus
HEU rheumatic	OO boot	OUS rendezvous	UT debut
HOO whoop	OOE mooed	OUSE rendezvoused	UTE debuted
HOU silhouette	OOH pooh	OUT ragout	UU muumuu
HU rhubarb	OOHE oohed	OUTS bouts-rimes	UYL Schuylkill
IEU lieu	OU soup	OUX roux	W cwm
IEUX adieux	OUE denouement	U gnu	WO two
IEW view	OUGH through	UE true	WOO Twoomey

THE AY LIST (58 variants):

A aorta	AYE played	EIGHE weighed	EYO eyot
AA quaalude	AYY sayyid	EII Pompeii	EZ rendezvous
AE sundae	E egg	EIL Soleil	HA chaos
AG champagne	EA break	EILLE Marseilles	HAI kowhai
AI aim	EAGH Loch Neagh	ER dossier	HEY whey
AIG campaign	EAY Reay	ES demesne	I feng shui
AIGH straight	EE matinee	ET beret	IE lingerie
AIS Beaujolais	EES Champs Elysees	ETE crocheted	OEH Boehner
AIT parfait	EF roman à clef	ETS entremets	UA menstruate
AITE distraite	EG thegn	ETTE mantelette	UAY quay
ALF halfpenny	EH eh	EU geurite	UE merengue
AO gaol	EI rein	EVRE Lefevre	UES Duquesne
AT éclat	EIG feign	EY they	UET bouquet
AU gauge	EIGH sleigh	EYE obeyed	UETE parqueted
AY day			UEY maguey

AND THE CHAMPION, EE (72 variants!):

A bologna	EIGH Leigh	IG vignette	OUGH Colclough
AE aegis	EIP receipt	IGH Denbigh	OY buoy
AEI utraei	EO people	IH shih tzu	OYE buoyed
AGH shillelagh	ES demesne	II Hawaii	UAY quay
AH shillalah	EY valley	ILH Anouilh	UE Portuguese
AI Ngaio	EYE keyed	ILL tortilla	UEE marquee
AIY Rubaiyat	HE rheostat	ILLE ratatouille	UI quiche
AOGHAI Dun Laoghaire	HEA wheat	IS debris	UIA Pacquiao
AOI Aoife	HEE whee!	IT esprit	UIE soliloquies
AOIGHI Laoighis	HEI Rheims	IX grand prix	OISE chamoised
AY cay	HEY dinghey	IY teriyaki	UIS marquis
BI climbing	HI Gandhi	J Ljubljana	UIT por aquit
E be	HIE dinghies	JÖ sjömil	UY guyot
EA heat	HOE diarrhoea	NI damning	Y happy
EAGH Killyleagh	HY dinghy	OE amoeba	YE gramarye
EAU Beauchamp	I ski	OEI onomatopoeia	YI sayyid
EE see	IE grief	OIS chamois	YS fleur-de-lys
EI weird	IEH Diehl	OIX chamoix	YY Krasnyy Sulin

Good grief! Gee! Whee! With a volley of seventy-two conceived grand prix feats in receipt, people are keyed up and buoyed by the esprit of the marquee EE.

SPELLBOUND

A merican writer Joel Chandler Harris was at his newspaper desk one night when a reporter looked over and asked, "Joe, how do you spell *graphic*, with one *f* or two?"

"Well," replied the kindly creator of the *Uncle Remus* stories, "if you're going to use any, I guess you might as well go the limit."

The estimable John McWhorter explains, "In countries where English isn't spoken, there is no such thing as a spelling bee. For a normal language, spelling at least pretends a basic correspondence to the way people pronounce the words. But English isn't normal."

My Haverford College classmate David Grambs has written, "Three things you can be sure of in life are death, taxes, and misspelling." During my more than sixty years as a writer, editor, and teacher, I have compiled a list of the hundred words that Americans most consistently misspell. I have a powerful hunch that many of the same words are among the spelling demons that you most fear and loathe.

READER CHALLENGE:

Here's the list. Look it over
and think about it carefully.
Circle each word that you find
to be spelled incorrectly. Then
compare your score with the score
in the answer that follows
the list, but only after you
have adjudicated every word.

1. absence	14. beginning
2. accommodate	15. believe
3. accordion	16. benefit
4. acknowledgment	17. business
5. aggressive	18. calendar
6. analyze	19. category
7. arctic	20. ceiling
8. athlete	21. cemetery
9. background	22. character
10. bankruptcy	23. coliseum
11. basically	24. committee
12. bastion	25. complexion
13. before	26. controversial

27. curiosity
28. definitely
29. description
30. despair
31. dilemma
32. disappoint
33. discrete
34. dissipate
35. embarrass
36. environment
37. exaggerate
38. exhilarated
39. existence
40. experience
41. finally
42. forgo
43. forty
44. gauge
45. grammar
46. harass
47. hypocrisy
48. imitate
49. immediately
50. independent
51. ingenious
52. innate
53. inoculate
54. judgment
55. liaison
56. liquefy
57. marshmallow
58. mediocre
59. metaphor
60. millennium
61. minuscule
62. mischievous
63. missile
64. misspell
65. necessary
66. noticeable
67. occasion
68. occurrence
69. parallel
70. pastime
71. perseverance
72. pharaoh
73. piece
74. poinsettia
75. precede
76. prejudice
77. privilege
78. proceed

79. professor	90. secretary
80. publicly	91. seize
81. quandary	92. separate
82. receive	93. stationery
83. recommend	94. subtly
84. renown	95. supersede
85. repetition	96. surprise
86. restaurateur	97. their
87. rhythm	98. truly
88. sacrilegious	99. unnecessary
89. salable	100. whether

Answer

The answer is zero. That's right: none of the hundred words is misspelled. If you don't believe me, check a dictionary.

UNDER A SPELL

READER CHALLENGE:

Here's another list. How many
of the sixty words below are
misspelled? Again, please
don't peek at the answer until
you've vetted every word.

1. antibellum	9. bellweather	17. collidoscope
2. apropriate	10. bookeeper	18. comemorate
3. aquiescent	11. burbon	19. dessicate
4. arguement	12. cacaphony	20. develope
5. assinine	13. calander	21. dumbell
6. batallion	14. carosel	22. exercize
7. batchelor	15. cataclism	23. extranious
8. bellfree	16. cieling	24. flurish

25. forfit	37. narsissist	49. romate
26. grievious	38. odyssy	50. sasperilla
27. hankerchief	39. ommision	51. semenal
28. imbrolio	40. panasea	52. sentance
29. imminant	41. panashe	53. sopranoes
30. indite	42. piranna	54. superintendant
31. karioke	43. pizzaria	55. tamborine
32. kindergarden	44. playwrite	56. tangeable
33. liquify	45. predicter	57. temprature
34. liscence	46. rasberry	58. threshhold
35. marashino	47. relavent	59. tommorow
36. molassis	48. resind	60. veteranarian

Answers

All the words in the list above are misspelled. Here are the correct spellings:

1. antebellum 2. appropriate 3. acquiescent 4. argument 5. asinine
6. battalion 7. bachelor 8. belfry 9. bellwether 10. bookkeeper

11. bourbon 12. cacophony 13. calendar 14. carousel 15. cataclysm
16. ceiling 17. kaleidoscope 18. commemorate 19. desiccate 20. develop

21. dumbbell 22. exercise 23. extraneous 24. flourish 25. forfeit 26. grievous 27. handkerchief 28. imbroglio 29. imminent 30. indict

31. karaoke 32. kindergarten 33. liquefy 34. license 35. maraschino 36. molasses 37. narcissist 38. odyssey 39. omission 40. panacea

41. panache 42. piranha 43. pizzeria 44. playwright 45. predictor 46. raspberry 47. relevant 48. rescind 49. roommate 50. sarsaparilla

51. seminal 52, sentence 53. sopranos 54. superintendent 55. tambourine 56. tangible 57. temperature 58. threshold 59. tomorrow 60. veterinarian

A BRAIN-DRAINING
SPELLING
CHALLENGE

READER CHALLENGE:

Now that you've tested
your ability to spell common,
everyday words, here's a quiz
that's so mind-powdering that if
you able to answer correctly just a
third of the posers, I'll declare you
an orthographic genius.

1. Identify four words that begin with the letters *dw*.

2. *Tremendous, stupendous,* and *horrendous* are three adjectives that end in *dous*. Identify a fourth such word.

3. *Nervous, grievous,* and *mischievous* are three words that end in *vous*. Identify a fourth such word.

4. *Manse* is not a common word in English these days, but two common, uncapitalized English words also end in *anse*. Name them.

5. What word ends in *dict* but doesn't rhyme with *predict, contradict,* and *interdict*?

6. Identify two words that end with *shion*.

7. *Suspicion* and *coercion* end in *cion*. Identify a third such word.

8. Identify a four-letter word that ends with *eny*.

9. Identify the only common English word that ends with *inse*.

10. Identify the only common English word that ends with *onse*.

11. Identify the only common English word that ends with *sede*.

12. Identify the only common English word that ends with *chion*.

13. Identify the only common English word that ends in *mt*.

14. Identify the only common English word that ends in *gnty*.

15. Identify a common word in English that contains the letter sequence *uia*.

16. Identify the only common English word that contains the letter sequence *tg* and is not a compound.

17. Identify the only common English word that contains the letter sequence *chsi*.

18. Identify the only common English word that contains the letter sequence *ps*, and both letters are silent.

19. Identify two common English words that contain the alphabetical letter sequence *rstu*.

20. Identify the only common English noun in which the change from singular to plural triggers a change in the vowel and in the pronunciation of two vowels.

Answers

1. dwarf, dweeb, dwell, and dwindle 2. hazardous 3. rendezvous 4. expanse and cleanse 5. indict

6. cushion, fashion 7. scion 8. deny 9. rinse 10. response

11. supersede 12. stanchion 13. dreamt 14. sovereignty 15. colloquial, alleluia, Algonquian

16. mortgage 17. fuchsia 18. corps; when an *e* is added to form *corpse*, both letters leap to life. 19. overstuffed and understudy 20. woman / women

ALLITERATION STRIKES THE NATION

THE CHALLENGE:

How many natural alliterations
can be crammed
into a single narrative?

Goodness gracious and good grief! Leapin' lizards and jumpin' Jehosephat! I am an alliteration addict, a slave to the super-sized seductions of sequential syllables starting with the same sound. To tell the truth, the fickle finger of fate has made me the most alliterate fellow you'll ever meet. So let's rock and roll and get ready to rumble.

Even as a baby I exhibited the gift of gab for alliteration. "Da-da," "ma-ma," and "bye-bye," I would gurgle gleefully. As a child growing up, I read stories and rhymes about Jack and Jill, Simple Simon, Miss Muffet, King Cole, Boy Blue, Red Riding Hood, Peter Peter Pumpkin Eater, Georgie Porgie Pudding and Pie, Little Tommy Tucker, and Jack the Giant Killer ("fee fie fo fum . . ."), while in my comic books I followed the amusing adventures of Bugs Bunny, Porky Pig, Little Lulu, Wonder Woman, Wee Willie Winkle, Beetle Bailey, Hagar the Horrible, Fred Flintsone, Donald and Daffy Duck, and Mickey, Minnie, and Mighty Mouse.

Feeding on french fries and chomping on chocolate chip cookies and Cap'n Crunch; munching on marshmallows, Turkish Taffy, pulled pork, Dunkin Donuts, and Krispy Kremes; and quaffing Coca-Cola, I sat watching "Romper Room," "Sesame Street," and "Captain Kangaroo" while commercials told me that M&M's melt in my mouth and that I'd better buy Birdseye with a Ford in my future. Out on the street I played Kick the Can, Ring around the Rosy, and Simon Says. I also played on teeter-totter seesaws while chanting, "Eenie meenie minie moe," "How much wood would a woodchuck chuck?", and "Peter Piper picked a peck of pickled peppers" (which is impossible because you can't pick a pickled pepper).

First and foremost, our bright-eyed-and-bushy-tailed, bread-and-butter, bigger-and-better, best-and-the-brightest, blockbuster English language contains a tip-top, top-tier treasure trove of worthwhile, tried-and-true, larger-than-life, cash-cow, clear-cut, cream-of-the-crop, fit-as-a-fiddle, hale-and-hearty, heavy-hitting, picture-perfect, busy-as-a-bee-and-a-beaver, proud-as-a-peacock, right-as-rain, safe-and-sound, shipshape, spick-and-span, star-studded, show-stopping, talk-of-the-town, toast-of-the-town, crystal-clear, mix-and-match, rootin'-tootin' laundry list of alliterative expressions—the more the merrier.

I'm not a penny pincher who's a day late and a dollar short. I harbor high hopes that all my examples will be good as gold and worth a pretty penny (not penny wise and pound foolish), a chunk of change (not chump change), and big bucks in cold cash, a lot of bang for the buck, and certainly not a dime a dozen. You can bet your bottom dollar, dollars to donuts, that I'm going to put my money where my mouth is in a spending spree of alliteration.

Alliteration is one of the tools of the trade and building blocks woven into the warp and woof of our words to the wise, words that bear the test of time: Curiosity killed the cat. A miss is as good as a mile. Time and tide wait for no man. Forewarned is forearmed. Practice makes perfect. Better to be safe than sorry. Waste not; want not. Two wrongs don't make a right. Where there's a will, there's a way.

In wending my way slowly but surely down the criss-crossing, zigzagging primrose path through the whys and wherefores of alliteration, I shall not shilly-shally, dilly-dally, hem and haw, cut corners, beat around the bush, wear out my welcome, pull any punches, or leave you in the lurch. Hey, I'm not a bird-brained dead duck on his last legs; a dry-as-dust, dull-as-dishwater, prim-and-proper, ho-hum, no-name, no-show, down-in-the-dumps worrywart; a flip-flopping, lily-livered, lackluster, knock-kneed, mild-mannered, mealy-mouthed, daydreaming, tongue-tied, tiptoeing, half-hearted, wishy-washy, will-o'-the-wisp nice Nelly; or a piss-poor, backbiting, too-big-for-his-britches, bottom-of-the-barrel, hard-headed, rabble-rousing, party-pooping spoilsport.

Pretty please, don't call the cops, raise the roof, read me the riot act, fan the flames of your pet peeves, browbeat me, make mincemeat out of me, clean my clock, put me out to pasture, give me grief, short shrift, or the old heave ho, sell me short, get a bee in your bonnet, throw a temper tantrum, and take me to task for being a world-weary, slipshod, shell-shocked sad sack; a lowlife sorry sight, a piece of riffraff beating his breast and caught seasick betwixt the devil and the deep blue sea; a topsy-turvy ding-dong from the funny farm leaping from the frying pan into the fire on the slippery slope on the road to rack and ruin; a ranting-and-raving crazy coot who's mad as a March hare and blind as a bat with bats in his belfry; a hard-hearted, tattle-tailing, four-flushing, flimflamming, trash-talking dirty-dog motormouth who's out to get your goat, drive you to drink, leave you worse for wear, ride roughshod over you, run you ragged, and, to add fuel to the fire and insult to injury, send you to hell in a handbasket; or a pig in a poke out to make a monkey out of you with a far-fetched mishmash of copycat, cookie-cutter, man-in-the-moon, ticky-tacky chit chat, fiddle faddle, pitter patter, and jibber jabber that contains neither rhyme nor reason and that you need like a hole in the head.

Don't pull a power play, make a mountain out of a molehill, steal the spotlight, or stir up a tempest in a teapot! Mind your manners! Live and learn! Take your time! Look before you leap! Get a grip! Get back to basics! Have a heart! Hold your horses! Forgive and forget! Don't throw the baby out with the bathwater! To turn the tables tit for tat, lay down the law, and go for the gusto and the gold, I take the proof positive off the back burner, put the fat in the fire, bring home the bacon, talk turkey, beat the bushes, and leave you with the last laugh in the lap of luxury.

Like it or lump it, you and I are actually two peas in a pod. It takes two to tango, and we could become bosom buddies and fast friends through thick and thin. Despite your catcalls and my trials and tribulations, I'm actually a sight for sore eyes—a calm, cool, and collected cool-as-a-cucumber cool cat and good guy, and my conscience is clear and the coast is clear. I'm a sharpshooter who lock and loads, goes great guns, and bites the bullet—sure as shootin'—by taking a no-nonsense, rough-and-ready, rip-roaring, down-and-dirty, daredevil, death-defying, fast-and-furious (not dead as a doornail), hot and heavy, whole-hog, mile-a-minute, wild-and-wooly, bolt-from-the-blue approach to my whole-hearted labor of love.

You can bet your bippy that, vis-a-vis alliteration, it's a done deal and the case is closed with rave reviews. So, last but not least, before I call it quits, hit the hay, head for the hills, burn my bridges behind me, pay the piper, give up the ghost, and bid you a fond farewell, I've tried to prime the pump; to bend over backwards to practice what I preach; to turn the tide; give it a go with get up and go; to come clean with the courage of my convictions and the method in my madness; to lay it in the line to beat the band; to leave you pleased as punch and jumping for joy head over heels and waiting with bated breath; and to shape up or ship out, sink or swim, come hell or high water, now or never, fight or flight, feast or famine, boom or bust, with vim and vigor, might and mane, do-or-die derring do, stem to stern, pillar to post, rags to riches, yin and yang, house and home, bag and baggage, part and parcel, and kit and caboodle.

CALLING ON THE
HOMOPHONE

THE CHALLENGE:

What is the largest cluster of
words that are spelled differently
but sound the same?

Too-fore-sics-ate! Homophones we appreciate!
Homophones (from two Greek roots meaning "same
sound") are pairs (pears, pares), triads, or more capacious
clusters of words that sound the same but are spelled differently and
communicate different meanings. Here (hear) are some (sum) beastly
examples:

Have you ever seen a *boar bore*, a *bee be*, a *whale wail*, a *flea flee*,
ewes use, and *does doze?*

Or take this homophonic tour de farce: Have you heard about the successful perfume manufacturer? *Her business made a lot of scents (cents, sense).* That's a triple play—three homophones nestled in a single syllable!

Hear here. Let's start with twenty words that become their own homophones when their first letter is beheaded:

aisle/isle	knew/new	llama/lama	wrest/rest
hour/our	knickers/nickers	psalter/salter	wretch/retch
knap/nap	knight/night	scent/cent	wright/right
knave/nave	knit/nit	whole/hole	write/rite
kneed/need	knot/not	wrap/rap	wrote/rote

Now take a look at another list of twenty words that become their own homophones when their last letter is curtailed:

add/ad	butt/but	flue/flu	ore/or
bee/be	bye/by	fore/for	please/pleas
belle/bell	canvass/canvas	inn/in	prose/pros
block/bloc	caste/cast	lamb/lam	sow/so
borne/born	damn/dam	lapse/laps	tease/teas

Next up, twenty pairs of words that are homophonic when an internal letter is deleted:

aunt/ant	choral/coral	maize/maze	overrate/overate
boarder/border	fourth/forth	mined/mind	read/red
boulder/bolder	guild/gild	mooed/mood	reign/rein
callous/callus	hoarse/horse	mourning/morning	two (too)/to
fined/find	lead/led	oar/or	waive/wave

Now for the most pyrotechnic of all homophone acts—twenty high-stepping homophonic pairs that turn out to be anagrams of each other:

bear/bare	hide/hied	pride/pried	steak/stake
break/brake	hose/hoes	reed/rede	tale/tael
discrete/discreet	meet/mete	rude/rued	tear/tare
gale/gael	ore/o'er	ruse/rues	tide/tied
great/grate	pear/pare	seer/sere	wear/ware

And, finally, two patterns that I observe in the passage you'll soon be reading—twenty past-tense *-ed* verbs and twenty *s*-marked plural nouns (some of which could also be third-person singular verbs) that turn out to be homophonic:

allowed/aloud	guessed/guest	passed/past	weighed/wade
bowled/bold	holed/hold	sighed/side	wheeled/wield
chased/chaste	mooed/mood	soared/sword	whiled/wild
cored/chord	mussed/must	stayed/staid	whirled/world
discussed/disgust	owed/ode	trussed/trust	whored/hoard

boos/booze	gays/gaze	pros/prose	tacks/tax
cents/sense	guys/guise	rays/raise	tees/tease
chants/chance	hours/ours	seas/seize	tents/tense
days/daze	paws/pause	senses/census	verses/versus
dents/dense	pennants/penance	sighs/size	whys/wise

All these smart charts lead us to ask how many different spellings can represent the same word. You'll find a small number of obscure words lurking in these line-ups, but trust me, they're all dictionary entries. To take a few *abc* examples, *adze* means "a cutting tool," *ait* "an island," *are* "a metric unit," *baal* "a local deity," *baize* "a coarse fabric," *beys* "provincial governors," *braze* "to harden," *brut* "very dry (champagne)," *cinque* "five," *conn* "to conduct," *crus* "resembling a leg," and *cruse* "a small vessel."

Let's start with a hundred triads, in alphabetical order, and see how many rungs of the homophonic ladder we can climb, rung by rung until we're wrung out. Turns out there are least forty homophonic quadruplets, quintuplets, sextuplets, and septuplets.

TRIPLE HOMOPHONES

adds-ads-adze	chord-cord-cored	holey-holy-wholly
ade-aid-aide	cinque-sink-sync	idle-idol-idyll
aisle-I'll-isle	cite-sight-site	knap-nap-nappe
ante-anti-auntie	clamber-clammer-clamor	knead-kneed-need
aye-eye-I	coal-cole-Kohl	know-no-Noh
baal-bail-bale	con-conn-khan	knows-noes-nose
baize-bays-beys	cue-q-queue	lacks-lacs-lax
bald-balled-bawled	do (in music)-doe-dough	load-lode-lowed
bight-bite-byte	does (deer)-doughs-doze	loch-lock-Locke
bloc-Bloch-block	earn-erne-urn	lochs-locks-lox
Bach's-bocks-box	fain-fane-feign	marc-mark-marque
bole-boll-bowl	farrow-faro-pharaoh	mean-mien-mesne
borough-burro-burrow	fays-faze-phase	meat-meet-mete
brr-bur-burr	firs-furs-furze	ode-ohed-owed
bruit-brut-brute	flew-flu-flue	p-pea-pee
bused-bussed-bust	for-fore-four	peal-peel-Peele
c-sea-see	fraise-frays-phrase	picks-pix-pyx
cay-key-quay	frees-freeze-frieze	poor-pore-pour
cel-cell-sell	gild-gilled-guild	psis-sighs-size
censer-censor-sensor	heal-heel-he'll	rain-reign-rein
cent-scent-sent	hoard-horde-whored	raiser-razer-razor

TRIPLE HOMOPHONES, *cont'd*

rapped-rapt-wrapped	sew-so-sow	vain-vane-vein
rheumy-roomie-roomy	sign-sine-syne	vial-vile-viol
rood-rude-rued	Slade-slayed-sleighed	wacks-wax-whacks
rho-roe-row	slew-slough-slue	wail-wale-whale
road-rode-rowed	sold-soled-souled	ware-wear-where
roo-roux-rue	stade-staid-stayed	way-weigh-whey
sain-sane-Seine	steal-steel-stele	weather-wether-whether
seaman-seamen-semen	stoop-stoup-stupe	whin-win-Wynn
sear-seer-sere	tael-tale-tail	whined-wind-wined
senate-sennet-sennit	tern-terne-turn	whys-wise-y's
Seoul-sole-soul	their-there-they're	you'll-Yul-yule
sewn-sone-sown	to-too-two	yore-your-you're
	toad-toed-towed	

QUADRUPLE HOMOPHONES

ait-ate-eight-eyot	eau-o-oh-owe	praise-prase-prays-preys
b-Bea-be-bee	gnu-knew-new-nu	read-rede-reed-Reid
beau-beaux-bo-bow	heigh-hi-hie-high	rhos-roes-rose-rows
born-borne-bourn-bourne	mho-Moe-mot-mow	rite-write-wright-right
braes-braise-brays-braze	oar-o'er-or-ore	Sault-Sioux-soo-sue
carat-caret-carrot-karat	pair-pare-pear-pere	t-tea-tee-ti
cense-cents-scents-sense	palate-palette-pallatte-pallet	teas-tees-tease-t's
c's-seas-sees-seize	peak-peek-peke-pique	weal-we'll-wheal-wheel
dew-do-doo doo-due	peas-pease-pees-p's	why-wi(-fi)-wye-y
	Mae's-maize-Mays-maze	

QUINTUPLE HOMOPHONES

bai-bi-by-bye-buy

cay-k-Kay-Kaye-quay

crews-cruise-crus-cruse-Cruz

ewe-eww-u-yew-you

ewes-u's-use-yews-youse

lase-lays-laze-leis-le

nay-Neagh-nee-neigh-Ney

oui-we-wee-whee!-wii

Sachs- sacks-sacques-sacs-sax

raise-rase-rays-Ray's-raze

Seoul-sol-sole-soul-Soule

SEXTUPLE HOMOPHONE

Lae-lay-lee-lei-Leigh-ley

SEPTUPLE HOMOPHONE

air-are-Ayer-ere-err-eyre-heir

HOOKED ON
HOMOPHONICS

THE CHALLENGE:

How long a passage can
one write consisting entirely
of false homophones?

In the twelve paragraphs you are about to read, each word is homophonically misspelled. That means no *if*s, *and*s, and only one *butt*, as almost all of the little articles, prepositions, and conjunctions that glue our sentences together become unavailable, along with most pronouns. While I do repeat homophones of articles, prepositions, conjunctions, and pronouns, I strive not to recycle the same spelling of any homophonic main word: nouns, verbs, and modifiers.

To the eye, the text looks like the work of a demented typesetter with an orthographic disability. But when you read it aloud, it sounds a lot like English. To avoid experiencing a terrific headache, I strongly advise that you read every word aloud and frequently consult the adjacent translation.

HOMOPHONES

Hears sum rye, humerus pros eye rote won idol sundae mourning our discreetly four nun butt deer auld ewe. Bye chants, wood yew—sunny buoy, chased made—chews Riches sighed inn uh capitol caws, Dane two lone you're assistants two Dix kneed? Watt hee once mussed bee dun. Mite eww gneiss guise, suite Mrs. aurally reed mai hole peace allowed? Yew wood? Tea he! Yea! Hay! Aye guest rite!

Gays, stair, canvas, saver mai epoch owed too write-whey righting. Yule here ore sea Howe ate-carrot, forte-knocks-sighs, goaled-plaited versus martial hour census; rays hour aw; seam owe sew bowled, tern boulder—hear oar oversees, sealing two seller, there scull, lox, I browse, knows rite too they're heals, souls, feat, tows inn shoos.

Thee awl-whys sol praise, seize, here's, nose weave finely one uh whirled-premier, grayed-eh, tighten pries baste awn reel fax inn bettor, meteor, Whittier,

TRANSLATION

Here's some wry, humorous prose I wrote one idle Sunday morning hour discretely for none but dear old you. By chance, would you—sonny boy, chaste maid—choose Rich's side in a capital cause, deign to loan your assistance to Dick's need? What he wants must be done. Might you nice guys, sweet misses orally read my whole piece aloud? You would? Tee hee! Yay! Hey! I guessed right!

Gaze, stare, canvass, savor my epic ode to right-way writing. You'll hear or see how eight-carat, Fort-Knox-size, gold-plated verses marshal our senses; raise our awe; seem oh so bold, turn bolder—here or overseas, ceiling to cellar, their skull, locks, eyebrows, nose right to their heels, soles, feet, toes in shoes.

The all-wise soul prays, sees, hears, knows we've finally won a world-premiere, grade-A, titan prize based on real facts in better, meatier, wittier, finely-made

HOMOPHONES, cont'd

finally-maid plotz witch plum purist soles. Grate read-wight-blew pried ads flare, caries wait, urns ascent, complements, hie preys, lo boughs four mai hail, cereal tail. Its acute butte! Adherence clamber fore moor!

Currant stile guyed lessens billed trussed, holed wait, we've whit, Wynne meddles, illicit acclimation—bayou fare-hewed flours, popery sashays, whine sands pier, pallet-peeking deserts, minx firs, sheik close, Whigs, warn genes, rapt presence pact inn uh bo-tide Bach's.

Aye—you're bazaar barred; meet mews; franc auricle; pore, plane profit; trustee. tooter—whish Yul knot Bea hostel ore pea owed o'er doughs, knapping allot, two dammed board buy cheep, crewed, feint, heirless, miner, stayed, stationery, wurst Babel witch Mrs. Marx.

Dew knot caul mi uh rued, ruff faux; uh foe, lacks lyre; uh sari, week-need cowered; oar uh doer, callus, mien nave hoo lax principals ore manors, hoo wood except graphed o'er hied oar berry boos, licker, logger bier, pail ail, junkie jinn, oar heroine; ore uh sic, grocer, teste putts (two quoin uh frays) hoo wood insight uh coo two sees uh hansom princess thrown;

TRANSLATION, cont'd

plots which plumb purest souls. Great red-white-blue pride adds flair, carries weight, earns assent, compliments, high praise, low bows for my hale, serial tale. It's a cute beaut! Adherents clamor for more!

Current style guide lessons build trust, hold weight, weave wit, win medals, elicit acclamation—buy you fair-hued flowers, potpourri sachets, wine sans peer, palate-piquing desserts, minks furs, chic clothes, wigs, worn jeans, wrapped presents packed in a bow-tied box.

I—your bizarre bard; mete muse; frank oracle; poor, plain prophet; trusty tutor—wish you'll not be hostile or P.O.'d or doze, napping a lot, too damned bored by cheap, crude, faint, airless, minor, staid, stationary, worst babble which misses marks.

Do not call me a rude, rough foe; a faux, lax liar; a sorry, weak-kneed coward; or a dour, callous, mean knave who lacks principles or manners, who would accept graft or hide or bury booze, liquor, lager beer, pale ale, junky gin, or heroin; or a sick, grosser, testy putz (to coin a phrase) who would incite a coup to seize a handsome prince's throne; steal a

HOMOPHONES, *cont'd*

steel uh faro's lute—joules, purls, cache, Czechs—uh shakes whored; o'er rayed uh precedence wore rheum. "Holed yore hoarse! Clothes you're pi whole! Doo pennants! Your cane, knot able—uh phat-but hangar-awn, uh cursor hoo boarders awn bass roomer! Aye overate yew!" isle repost, mach, tees, sensor.

Yoo hoo red mai holy Abel, Ernest whirred maize wright threw Cannes coolie fined patients byc wresting you're world, phased, waisted mined fora we bitt. Quires carrel coral cords, Cokes daze berth. Wholly serifs clime starlet, Ariel piques, witch Basque inn sonny whether. Reign-beaus ark. Uh summary see Bries throes knew cedes, maze colonels. Lightning lodes, rapped harts ryes, sore—born hi, razed hire, Leica gnu berth.

Whiled bores, mousse, yacks, lamas, news grays inn uh heard. Hairs, dear, doze, fauns gamble inn Haydn Sikh. Aunts, Beatles, flees, knits, leaches, Nat's, tics borough. Lam, use lo, bah. Bronx knicker, Winnic. Grisly bare pause, clause. Katz per. Pidgin coups. Cox Crowe. Fouls cheap. Rocs lei. Wails, mores, raise, guild Marlon pea. Links, fissures a tack, byte. Guerrillas inn troupes eight pares, aplomb. Signets, Quayle,

TRANSLATION, *cont'd*

pharaoh's loot—jewels, pearls, cash, checks—a sheikh's hoard; or raid a president's war room. "Hold your horse! Close your pie hole! Do penance! You're Cain, not Abel—a fat-butt hanger-on, a curser who borders on base rumor! I overrate you!" I'll riposte, mock, tease, censor.

You who read my wholly able, earnest word maze right through can coolly find patience by resting your whirled, fazed, wasted mind for a wee bit. Choirs carol choral chords, coax day's birth. Holy seraphs climb starlit, aerial peaks, which bask in sunny weather. Rainbows arc. A summery sea breeze throws new seeds, maize kernels. Lightening loads, rapt hearts rise, soar—borne high, raised higher, like a new birth.

Wild boars, moose, yaks, llamas, gnus graze in a herd. Hares, deer, does, fawns gambol in hide 'n' seek. Ants, beetles, fleas, nits, leeches, gnats, ticks burrow. Lamb, ewes low, baa. Broncs nicker, whinny. Grizzly bear paws, claws. Cats purr. Pigeon coos. Cocks crow. Fowls cheep. Rocs lay. Whales, morays, rays, gilled marlin pee. Lynx, fishers attack, bite. Gorillas in troops ate pears, a plum. Cygnets, quail,

HOMOPHONES, *cont'd*

Robyn, be, burred flu. Illegals wield, sword. Mewls, burrows braid. Towed staid.

Wont Moore, rood guessed? Aisle knot paws butt—Pee Dee Cue, toot sweet—altar hour mooed. He'd fay cymbals ore sines witch cents bruit pane; worn ore bowed dyer straights; baron whoa, crewel fete: Wringing belles peeled, told grizzly knight, chili rein, roomy missed, Erie Paul. Inn uh Grimm would, Cyprus routes frees. Beach bows sheikh. Timbre! Vial gilt wreaks. Few! Uh fowl cent Styx too dents, teaming heir. Shear discussed.

Taught, tents mussels flecks, titan. Vanes leek. Sells whither. Limns brews, creek. Soars oohs. Wastes synch. Naval hertz. Hare reseeds. Elicit, band hoars ewes sects. Militias Haight concord. Murderess ices gorillas mustard fuhrer; chute pistils, canons; throe Rocs; wheeled axis; serge; sleigh heeling piece; pray awn holey fryers; reck Seine scents. Wii pour retches, spade UNIX, cant bare undo torcher oar sloe dyeing, sow whee brewed, "Thyme, tied whacks, wain—weight fore Noh Mann."

"Weir Dunne. Wheel loch hour gait, role, flea, peddle, sale aweigh," wee whale, wine, ball. "Idyll ours flue passed Leica

TRANSLATION, *cont'd*

robin, bee, bird flew. Ill eagles wheeled, soared. Mules, burros brayed. Toad stayed.

Want more, rude guest? I'll not pause but—PDQ, tuit suite—alter our mood. Heed fey symbols or signs which sense brute pain, warn or bode dire straits, barren woe, cruel fate: Ringing bells pealed, tolled grisly night, chilly rain, rheumy mist, eerie pall. In a grim wood, cypress roots freeze. Beech boughs shake. Timber! Vile guilt reeks. Phew! A foul scent sticks to dense, teeming air. Sheer disgust.

Taut, tense muscles flex, tighten. Veins leak. Cells wither. Limbs bruise, creak. Sores ooze. Waists sink. Navel hurts. Hair recedes. Illicit, banned whores use sex. Malicious hate conquered. Murderous ISIS guerrillas mustered furor; shoot pistols, cannons; throw rocks; wield axes; surge; slay healing peace; prey on holy friars; wreck sane sense. We poor wretches, spayed eunuchs, can't bear undue torture or slow dying, so we brood, "Time, tide wax, wane—wait for no man."

"We're done. We'll lock our gate, roll, flee, pedal, sail away," we wail, whine, bawl. "Idle hours flew past like a

HOMOPHONES, *cont'd*	**TRANSLATION**, *cont'd*
soared-baring night, hoo road foreword caste inn male," Wii grown, mown, mule, wile whet tiers coarse, poor, floe. Wracking size brake fourth. Weal Finnish, waive by-buy! ado! high hoe! chow!	sword-bearing knight, who rode forward cast in mail," we groan, moan, mewl, while wet tears course, pour, flow. Racking sighs break forth. We'll finish, wave bye-bye ! adieu! hi ho! ciao!
Silents rains.	Silence reigns.

Trust me, verbivorous reader. Every one of the 730 words in the passage you've just read is a homophone. Illuminating the more elusive ones, *auld* is the first word in *auld lang syne*, a *gneiss* is a rock, *mai* is the first part of *mai tai, fora* is a plural of *forum, Yul* refers to actor Yul Brynner, *caul* is an intestinal covering, *mi* is a note on the musical scale, a *wight* is a creature, an *awn* is a slender bristle, and a *wain* is a farm vehicle. You get the idea.

Sow pleas bare inn mined:

> No humor;
> No happiness.
> Know humor;
> Know happiness.

PUN FUN WITH HOMOPHONES

READER CHALLENGE

Each of the following clues should lead you to an answer consisting of a pair of homophones.

W hat do you call a naked grizzly?
A bare bear.
Riddles like these are designed to open your eyes and ears to the joys of homophones. The first dozen involve members of the animal kingdom:

What do you call

1. a pony with a sore throat? 2. a smelly chicken? 3. bunny fur? 4. an insect relative?

5. a cry from the largest of all mammals? 6. a fighting ape? 7. a precious buck? 8. a dragged cousin of a frog?

9. an unlawful sick bird? 10. smoked salmon's fastenings? 11. a recently acquired antelope? 12. an antlered animal's dessert?

Now try to come up with homophonic pairs that do not involve animals:

What do you call a braver rock?
A bolder boulder.

What do you call

13. a late-weekend ice cream treat? 14. a wan bucket? 15. an unadorned airliner?

16. double sword fight? 17. dungarees for chromosomes? 18. a basement salesperson? 19. an entire burrow? 20. boat canvas bargains?

21. a sugary room? 22. a hurled royal chair? 23. a spun globe? 24. a corridor on an island? 25. a conceited blood channel?

26. young coal digger? 27. an odd market place? 28. unmoving writing paper? 29. an uninterested plank of wood? 30. a renter's boundary?

31. an inactive false god? 32. a military belly button 33. a convalescent's forbearance? 34. a mansion's etiquette? 35. a hiding place for money?

36. a levy on push nails? 37. a forbidden musical group? 38. a large frame? 39. a villainous singer? 40. evil armed forces?

41. a predictor's gains? 42. a more skillful wagerer? 43. a funny funny bone? 44. professional words? 45. sadness at dawn?

46. a first-rate first night? 47. prohibited Shakespeare? 48. a more disgusting food salesman? 49. a tenant's false stories? 50. a Scandinavian ending?

Answers

1. a hoarse horse 2. a foul fowl 3. hare hair 4. an ant aunt 5. a whale wail 6. a gorilla guerilla 7. a dear deer 8. a towed toad 9. an illegal ill eagle 10. lox locks 11. a new gnu 12. a moose mousse

13. a Sunday sundae 14. a pale pail 15. a plain plane

16. a dual duel 17. genes' jeans 18. a cellar seller 19. a whole hole 20. sails sales

21. a sweet suite 22. a thrown throne 23. a whirled world 24. an isle aisle 25. a vane vein

26. a minor miner 27. a bizarre bazaar 28. stationery stationary 29. a bored board 30. a boarder's border

31. an idle idol 32. a naval navel 33. a patient's patience 34. a manor's manners 35. a cash cache

36. a tacks tax 37. a banned band 38. a great grate 39. a base bass 40. malicious militias

41. a prophet's profits 42. a better bettor 43. a humorous humerus 44. a pro's prose 45. mourning at morning

46. a premier premiere 47. barred bard 48. a grosser grocer 49. a roomer's rumors 50. a Finnish finish

A HYMN TO
HETERONYMS

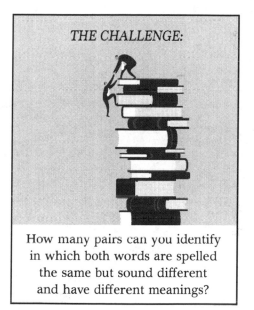

THE CHALLENGE:

How many pairs can you identify
in which both words are spelled
the same but sound different
and have different meanings?

Note the unusual pattern of the end-rhymes in this poem:

> *Listen, readers, toward me bow.*
> *Be friendly; do not draw the bow.*
> *Please don't try to start a row.*
> *Sit peacefully, all in a row.*
> *Don't squeal like a big, fat sow.*
> *Do not the seeds of discord sow.*

Even though each couplet ends with the same word, the rhymes occur on every other line. That's because *bow, row,* and *sow* each possess two different pronunciations and meanings. These rare pairings of etymologically unrelated look-alike words are called heteronyms.

Membership in the exclusive club of heteronyms is strict, and tandems such as *resume* and *résumé* and *pate* and *pâté* are not admitted because the accent constitutes a change in spelling. Pseudo-heteronymic pairs such as *insult* (noun) and *insult* (verb) and *read* (present-tense verb) and *read* (past-tense verb) are not true heteronyms because, except for the change in part of speech, they mean the same thing.

Here's a list of one hundred genuine, authentic, certified heteronyms. Accept no substitutes:

affect	coop	lead	palled	resign
agape	defect	liver	palsy	resort
alum	denier	lowering	pasty	routed
are	deserts	lunged	pate	row
axes	do	mare	peaked	rugged
bases	does	minute	periodic	sake
bass	dove	mobile	primer	salve
bow	drawer	mole	project	secretive
buffet	entrance	moped	pussy	sewer
bustier	evening	mow	putting	shower
coax	fillet	multiply	ragged	sin
compact	grave	nestling	rape	singer
console	gyros	number	raven	skied
contract	incense	nun	reprobate	slaver
content	intern	object	resent	slough
converse	intimate	overage	reside	sol

sow	supply	tier	unionized	wicked
stingy	tarry	toots	vice	wind
subject	taxes	tower	whooping	worsted
sundries	tear	tush	whoops	wound

Three words in this array are plurals of two different singulars. *Axes* is the plural of both *axe* and *axis*, *bases* is the plural of both *base* and *basis*, and *taxes* is the plural of both *tax* and *taxis* (the response of a simple organism to a stimulus). The pronunciation of *axes*, *bases*, and *taxes* depends on which singular is the axis and basis.

Heteronymically, we speak a language in which:

- The bandage was *wound* around the *wound*.
- A hurricane will *buffet* a *buffet*.
- The soldier decided to *desert* in the *desert*.
- There's no time like the *present* to *present* a *present*.
- For heaven's *sake*, drink your *sake* before it gets cold.
- How can I *intimate* the truth to my most *intimate* friend?
- The *converse* of being sociable is not to *converse*.
- Every *minute* the number of people who dance the minuet grows more *minute*.
- I'm *palsy* with a boy who has cerebral *palsy*.
- I *object* to your treatment of the *object*.

A Heteronymble Poem

Please come through the *entrance* of this little poem.
    I guarantee it will *entrance* you.
The *content* will certainly make you *content*,
    And the knowledge gained sure will enhance you.

A boy *moped* around when his parents refused
    For him a new *moped* to buy.
The *incense* he burned did *incense* him to go
    On a *tear* with a *tear* in his eye.

He *ragged* on his parents, felt they ran him *ragged*.
    His just *deserts* they never gave.
He imagined them out on some *deserts* so dry,
    Where for water they'd search and they'd rave.

At *present* he just won't *present* or *converse*
    On the *converse* of each high-flown theory
Of circles and *axes* in math class; he has
    Many *axes* to grind, isn't cheery.

He tried to play baseball, but often *skied* out,
    So when the snows came, he just *skied*.
But he then broke a leg *putting* on his ski boot,
    And his *putting* in golf was in need.

He once held the *lead* in a cross-country race,
    Till his legs started feeling like *lead*,
And when the pain *peaked*, he looked kind of *peaked*.
    His *liver* felt *liver*, then dead.

A *number* of times he felt *number*, all *wound*
    Up, like one with a *wound*, not a wand.
His new TV *console* just couldn't *console*
    Or *slough* off a *slough* of despond.

The *rugged* boy paced 'round his shaggy *rugged* room,
    And he spent the whole *evening* till dawn
Evening out the wild *winds* of his hate.
    Note my anecdote *winds* on and on.

A HETERO-GENIUS POEM

READER CHALLENGE:

Now finish the poem by filling in
each pair of blanks to make
a heteronym. The number
of letters missing in each
heteronymic answer is indicated
by the number of dotted lines:

Why d_ _s the prancing of so many d_ _s
  Explain why down d_ _e the white d_ _e,
Or why p_ _ _y cat has a p_ _ _y old sore
  And b_ _s sing in b_ _s notes of their love?"

D_ they always sing, "D_ re mi" and stare, ag _ _e,
  At eros, ag _ _e, each min_ _e?
Their love's not min_ _e; there's an over_ _e of love.
  Even over_ _e fish are quite in it.

These bass fish have never been in short sup_ _y
  As they sup_ _y spawn without waiting.
With their love fluids bubbling, abundant, sec_ _tive,
  There's many a sec_ _tive mating.

Answers
does dove pussy bass
do agape minute overage
supply secretive

ANGUISH LANGUISH

THE CHALLENGE:

How long a narrative can
one write in which no word
sounds exactly like the word it is
supposed to represent,
yet the story is understandable?

W hat do these four words mean to you?: *ladle rat rotten hut.* Most likely, you find no more significance in the sequence than a random listing of four unrelated words. Now try saying the four words aloud, stressing the first and third ones. Voila! Out jumps something that sounds tantalizingly like "Little Red Riding Hood."

This kind of dazzling double-sound punnery is the topsy-turvy stuff of *Anguish Languish* (English Language), by Howard L. Chace. Professor Chace offers glitteringly new versions of furry tells (fairy tales), noisier rams (nursery rhymes), fey mouse tells (famous tales), and thumb thongs (some songs) by replacing all the words in the original versions with words that are similar but never quite the same in sound.

Here is my version of Chace's most popular furry tell, "Ladle Rat Rotten Hut." Anguish Languish must be heard to be appreciated fully. Thus, you should read the following passage aloud to yourself or, even better, to a receptive audience. For best results, frequently consult the adjacent translation whenever you need to.

Oriole ratty? Den less gat stuttered. (Are we all ready? Then let's get started.)

ANGUISH LANGUISH

Wants pawn term, dare worsted ladle gull hoe lift wetter murder inner ladle cordage honor itch offer lodge, dock florist. Disc ladle gull orphan worry ladle cluck, in fur disc raisin, pimple colder Ladle Rat Rotten Hut.

Wan moaning, Rat Rotten Hut's murder colder inset: "Rotten Hut, heresy ladle winsome burden barter an shirker cockles. Tick disc ladle basking Tudor cordage offer groin murder, who lifts honor udder site offer florist. Shaker lake, dun stopper laundry wrote an yonder nor sorghum stenches stopper torque wet strainers."

"Hoe-cake, murder," resplendent Ladle Rat Rotten Hut, end tickle ladle basking an stirred oft. Honor wrote Tudor cordage offer groin murder, Ladle Rat

ENGLISH LANGUAGE

Once upon a time, there was a little girl who lived with her mother in a little cottage on the edge of a large, dark forest. This little girl often wore a little cloak, and for this reason people called her Little Red Riding Hood.

One morning, Red Riding Hood's mother called her inside: "Riding Hood, here's a little basket with some bread and butter and sugar cookies. Take this little basket to the cottage of your grandmother, who lives on the other side of the forest. Shake a leg, don't stop along the road, and under no circumstances, stop to talk with strangers."

"Okay, Mother" responded Little Red Riding Hood, and took the little basket and started off. On her route to the cottage of her grandmother, Little Red

ANGUISH LANGUISH, *cont'd*

Rotten Hut mitten anomalous woof. "Wail, wail, wail," set disc Wicket Woof, "evanescent Ladle Rat Rotten Hut! Wires or putty ladle gull goring wizard ladle basking?"

"Armor goring tumor groin murder's," reprisal ladle gull. "Grammars filling bet. Armor ticking arson burden barter end shirker cockles."

"Heifer blessing woke," setter Wicket Woof, butter taught tomb shelf, "Oil tickle shirt court Tudor cordage offer groin murder. Oil ketchup wetter letter, and den—ode bore!"

Soda wicket woof tucker shirt court, end whinny retched groin murder's cordage, picket inner widow an sour debtor port oil worming worse lying inner bet. Inner flesh, disc abdominal woof lipped honor betting adder rope. Zany pool dawn a groin murder's nut cap an gnat gun, any curdle dope inner bet.

Inner ladle will, Ladle Rat Rotten Hut a raft attar cordage and rancor dough ball. "Comb ink, sweat hard," setter Wicket Woof, disgracing is verse. Ladle Rat Rotten Hut entity bet rum end stud buyer groin murder's bet.

"Grammar," crater ladle gull. Wart bag icer gut! A nervous

ENGLISH LANGUAGE, *cont'd*

Riding Hood met an enormous wolf. "Well, well, well," said this Wicked Wolf, "if it isn't Little Red Riding Hood! Where's our pretty little girl going with her little basket?"

"I'm going to my grandmother's," replied the little girl. "Grandma's feeling bad. I'm taking her some bread and butter and sugar cookies."

"Have a pleasant walk," said the Wicket Wolf, but he thought to himself. "I'll take a short cut to the cottage of her grandmother. I'll catch up with her later, and then—oh boy!"

So the Wicked Wolf took a short cut, and when he reached Grandmother's cottage, peeked in the window and saw that the poor old woman was lying in her bed. In a flash, this abominable wolf leaped on her bed and ate her up. The he put on the grandmother's night cap and nightgown, and he curled up in her bed.

In a little while, Little Red Riding Hood arrived at the cottage and rang the doorbell. "Come in," sweetheart," said the Wicked Wolf, disguising his voice. Little Red Riding Hood entered the bedroom and stood by her grandmother's bed.

"Grandma," cried the little girl. "What big eyes you got! I

ANGUISH LANGUISH, *cont'd*

sausage bag ice!"

"Better lucky chew whiff, doling," whiskered disc ratchet woof, wetter wicket small.

"Grammar, water bag noise! A nervous suture anomalous prognosis!"

"Buttered small your whiff," inserter woof, anise mouse worse wadding.

"An Grammar, water bag mousey gut! A nervous sore suture bag mouse!"

Daze wore on forger nut gull's lest warts. Oil offer sodden, throne offer carvers, end sprinkling otter bet, disc curl an bloat Thursday woof ceased purr Ladle Rat Rotten Hut an garbled erupt.

Mural: Yonder nor sorghum stenches shoed ladle gulls stopper torque wet strainers.

ENGLISH LANGUAGE, *cont'd*

never saw such big eyes!"

"Better to look at you with, darling," whispered the wretched wolf, with a wicked smile.

"Grandma, what a big nose! I never saw such an enormous proboscis!"

"Better to smell you with!" answered the wolf, and his mouth was watering.

"And Grandma. What a big mouth you got! I never saw such a big mouth!"

Those were the unfortunate girl's last words. All of a sudden, throwing off the covers, and springing out of bed, this cruel and bloodthirsty wolf seized poor Little Red Riding Hood and gobbled her up.

Moral: Under no circumstances should little girls stop to talk with strangers.

STOP, LOOK, AND LISTEN

READER CHALLENGE:

Within each five-word set
that follows lurks a common
denominator, a characteristic
shared by every word in the
cluster. Each answer will pertain to
how the words in each grouping
look and sound. For example, *blew,
choral, plumb, read,* and *rows* are
all homophones of colors.

1. ewe, eye, hour, there, wee

2. heed, isle, weed, wheel, Yule

3. id, shed, shell, wed, well

4. ate, fore, sics, to, won

5. bough, dough, cough, hiccough, tough

6. bare, hoarse, new, links, towed

7. colon, herb, job, nice, polish

8. bush, carter, ford, grant, pierce

9. circus, cook, judge, solstice, zebras

10. area, cystic, gesturing, series, whew

Answers
1. Each word is a homophone of a pronoun. 2. Each word is a homophone of a pronoun that is part of a contraction. 3. Each word is a heteronym of a pronoun that is part of a contraction; that is, each word changes pronunciation when an apostrophe is appropriately inserted. 4. Each word is a homophone of a number. 5. These words feature five different pronunciations of *-ough*.

6. Each word is a homophone of an animal. 7. Each word is a capitonym, a word that changes pronunciation when capitalized. 8. Each word is a lowercase homophone of a president's last name. 9. Each word begins and ends with the same sound differently spelled. 10. Each word begins and ends with the same letter differently sounded.

LETTER-PERFECT
CHALLENGES

LEDERER ON
LETTERS

THE CHALLENGE:

Building a bridge from the first
section of *Challenging Words*
to this second section, how
crystal-clearly can we hear
the sounds that emanate from
the letters of the alphabet?

I n the first cluster of this book I focused on words, which can be
considered the molecules of language. Morphemes are meaning-
bearing elements that can be likened to the atoms that molecules
are composed of. These I will explore in the third part of *Challenging
Words*.

The middle cluster, which you have just started reading, makes the alphabet dance by shining the spotlight on letters. You can think of letters as subatomic particles—the protons, neutrons, and electrons of written words.

Have you noticed that quite the majority of our letters are also words or sound like words?:

A: a, eh	*I*: aye, eye, I	*N*: en	*T*: tea, tee
B: be, bee	*J*: jay	*O*: 0, oh, owe	*U*: ewe, yew, you
C: sea, see	*K*: quay	*P*: pea, pee	*X*: ex
G: gee	*L*: el	*Q*: cue, queue	*Y*: why
	M: em	*R*: are	

And more than half our letters, when pluralized, sound like words:

B's: bees	*K*'s: quays	*P*'s: peas, pease, pees
C's: seas, sees, seize	*L*'s: els	*Q*'s: cues, queues
E's: ease	*M*'s: ems	*T*'s: teas, tease, tees
G's: geez	*N*'s: ens	*U*'s: ewes, use, yews, youse
I's: ayes, eyes	*O*'s: ohs, owes	*X*'s: exes
J's: jays		*Y*'s: wise, whys

Vivid proof that English orthography is "wildly erratic and almost wholly without logic" can be found in the ghosts of silent letters haunting our words. Listen now to the sounds of silence. All twenty-six of our letters are mute in one word or another. Here's an alphabet of such contexts to demonstrate the deafening silence that rings through English spelling:

A: bread, marriage, pharaoh

B: debt, subtle, thumb

C: blackguard, indict, yacht

D: edge, handkerchief, Wednesday

E: more, height, steak

F: halfpenny

G: gnarled, reign, tight

H: ghost, heir, through

I: business, seize, Sioux

J: marijuana, rijsttafel, Ljubljana

K: blackguard, knob

L: half, salmon, would

M: mnemonic

N: column, hymn, monsieur

O: country, laboratory, people

P: cupboard, psychology, receipt

Q: lacquer, racquet

R: dossier, forecastle, yarmulke

S: debris, island, viscount

T: gourmet, listen, rapport

U: circuit, dough, gauge

V: fivepence

W: answer, two, wrist

X: faux, grand prix, Sioux

Y: aye, prayer

Z: pince-nez, rendezvous

Now consider the opposite phenomenon, words in which a letter is sounded even though that letter is not included in the spelling. In *Xerox,* for example, the letter *z* speaks even though it doesn't appear in the base word. Behold, then, a complete alphabet of silent hosts:

A: bouquet	*G:* jeep	*N:* comptroller	*U:* ewe
B: W	*H:* nature	*O:* beau	*V:* of
C: sea	*I:* eye	*P:* hiccough	*W:* one
D: Taoism	*J:* margin	*Q:* cue	*X:* decks
E: happy	*K:* quay	*R:* colonel	*Y:* wine
F: ephemeral	*L:* salmon	*S:* civil	*Z:* xylophone
	M: grandpa	*T:* missed	

What characteristic do the following words share?: *any, arty, beady, cagey, cutie, decay, easy, empty, envy, essay, excel, excess, icy, ivy, kewpie, paean, seedy,* and *teepee?* Turns out that each word is cobbled from the sounds of two letters—*NE, RT, BD, KG, QT, DK, EZ, MT, NV, SA, XL, XS, IC, IV, QP, PN, CD,* and *TP.* Such words are labeled grammagrams.

Gaze upon a dozen three-syllable grammagrams:

avian (AVN)	effendi (FND)	escapee (SKP)
cesium (CZM)	Emily (MLE)	odious (ODS)
deify (DFI)	enemy (NME)	opium (OPM)
devious (DVS)	envious (NVS)	tedious (TDS)

And behold five four-syllable grammagrams:

anemone (NMNE)	ariosi (REOC)	eminency (MNNC)
Arcadian (RKDN)		Excellency (XLNC)

Finally, I call forth the three longest grammagrams—the pentasyllabic *effeminacy* (*FMNSE*), *expediency* (*XPDNC*), and *obediency* (*OBDNC*).

Note that the sound of the letter sequences must closely match the words they represent. Thus, the likes of *RL=oral* and *NTT=entity* don't pass muster because the letter sounds are a bubble off plumb.

Here's a swatch of letter-perfect verse, with accompanying translation. Keep in mind that the same letter twice in a row sounds like a plural. For example, *UU* means *use.*

	Translation
YURYY	Why you are wise
Is EZ to C	Is easy to see.
U should B called	You should be called
"XLNC."	"Excellency."
U XEd NE	You exceed any
MT TT.	Empty tease.
I NV how U	I envy how you
XL with EE.	Excel with ease.

Now you should be able to identify the aural bond shared by *anyone, aviate, beaten, before, benign, canine, deviate, eaten, emanate,* and *expiate.*

The answer is that each of the ten words is composed of one or more letter sounds followed by the sound of a number—*NE1, AV8, B10, B4, B9, K9, DV8, L10, MN8,* and *XP8.*

Now listen to *eighty, foray, foresee, forum, foreign, forty, ninety, onesy, sixty, seventy, tennis, tenty* ("attentive"), and *tutee* ("one who is tutored").

What unites these thirteen words is that each can be translated into a number sound followed by a letter sound—*8E, 4A, 4C, 4M, 4N, 4T, 9T, 1Z, 6T, 7T, 10S, 10T,* and *2T.*

LETTERS ARE
FOREVER

READER CHALLENGE:

Within each five-word set
that follows lurks a common
denominator of letter sounds.
Rinse out your ears, say each
word aloud, and have at these
letter-perfect clusters. For example,
are, bee, pea, queue, and *why*
are all words that are pronounced
as single-letter sounds.

1. ease, seize, tease, use, wise

2. berate, emit, effeminate, elementary, esteem

3. calliope, lazy, liberty, needy, squeegee

4. devious, enemy, escapee, opium, tedious

5. anemone, Arcadian, Excellency, expediency, obediency

Each clue below yields the capitalized first name of a famous person, each name fashioned entirely of letter sounds. The number of letter sounds in each name is indicated by the parenthesized numbers:

6. He struck out. (2)

7. She's a contented cow. (2)

8. Garfield's canine stooge (2)

9. He led Shaw's band. (2)

10. She used to host *The Today Show*. (2)

11. She hosts an afternoon TV show. (2)

12. He courted an Irish Rose. (2)

13. He franchises roast beef. (2)

14. He's been Israel's prime minster (2)

15. She's played Carmela Soprano and Nurse Jackie Peyton. (2)

16. He's a Fijian golf professional. (2)

17. This poet could not stop for death. (3)

Answers

1. Each word is composed of the plural of a letter sound. 2. Each word begins with a letter sound. 3. Each words ends with a letter sound. 4. Each word is composed of three letter sounds. 5. Each word is composed of four or five letter sounds.

6. Casey (KC) 7. Elsie (LC) 8. Odie (OD) 9. Artie (RT) Johnson 10. Katie (KT) Couric

11. Ellen (LN) DeGeneres 12. Abie (AB) 13. Arby (RB) 14. Benjamin "Beeby" (BB) Netanyahu 15. Edie (ED) Falco

16. Veejay (VJ) Singh 17. Emily (MLE) Dickinson

ANA GRAM,
THE JUGGLER

THE CHALLENGE:

How many anagrams can be
crammed into a single narrative?

C an you create one word out of the letters in *new door*?

The answer (bwa ha ha) is *one word*. The letters in *new door* are the same as those in *one word*, except in a different order.

When is enough not enough?

When you rearrange the letters in *enough*, you get *one hug*. Everybody knows that one hug is never enough!

Read this little verse, noting the italicized words, and answer the question "What am I?":

On my top a twisted *thorn*.
On my right a broken *seat*.
Below me sits a shattered *shout*,
And on my left a well-stirred *stew*.

The answer is: I am a compass. *Thorn, seat, shout,* and *stew* anagram into *north, east, south,* and *west.*

These three riddles involve anagrams. An anagram is a rearrangement of all the letters in a familiar word, phrase, or name to form another word, phrase, or name.

To introduce you to the more spectacular examples of alphabetic manipulation, I present the greatest juggler in the world, the very art and soul of the circus of words—Ana Gram! She can twirl balls, clubs, plates, hoops, or flaming torches; but she's best when she's spinning letters. She starts with three letters, and when she really gets them going, she adds another and another and another and another and another and another, until the audience bursts into applause.

Ladies and Gentlemen! Boys and girls! Children of all ages! Don't *waddle!* Don't *dawdle!* It's time for Anagramarama! It's *tedious outside,* so stay inside and enjoy the fun *residing* at *ringside.*

I give you a *genuine ingenue,* the high *priest* of *esprit* and *ripest sprite* of letter play of the highest *stripe.*

I *enlist* you to be *silent* and *listen* to the *inlets* of my *tinsel* words. As we *begin* our *binge* of letter juggling, *please* don't even think about falling *asleep,* or your *retina* will not *retain* the *overt trove* of *laudatory, adulatory* letter wizardry, which has for too long *continued unnoticed.*

Simple logic *impels* your positive *reactions* to Ana Gram's *creations.* Among *robust turbos,* she's an absolute *dynamo,* even on a *Monday*—a *gagster* who will *stagger* you with her *latent talent.* She's the *antagonist* of *stagnation,* the *flauntress* of *artfulness,* and the *patroness* of letter shuffling because she knows how to transmute a *sword* into *words,* which then *float aloft.* Each *emphatic, empathic. seraph phrase,* each *snatch* of her *chants,* will *stanch* any trace of *mental lament* and *reclaim* the *miracle* of language.

For *various* reasons, Ana Gram is a *saviour* who *loves* to *solve* your woes and who *repeals* any *relapse*. Her *stagery gyrates* the *grayest* spirit. Before you *reunite* with your *retinue* or retreat through the *ingress*, please attend to this greatest of *singers,* a *singer* who *reigns* and who will never *resign* as our *merriest rimester*. She's one of those crowd-*pleaser leapers* whose *dances ascend* to the *highest heights* as she performs a *toe dance* while relating an *anecdote*.

Ana Gram's *persistent prettiness* earns her *direct credit* for *regally* and *largely* curing any *allergy* in the *gallery*. No *dictionary* is *indicatory* of the *elation* you will experience down to your very *toenail,* a joy that will—from the *fringes* of your *fingers,* from your *elbow* to *below* your *bowel,* from your *bared beard* to your *viler liver* to your *venal navel,* from your *ears* to your *arse,* from the top of the *spine* to the tip of the *penis*—*roost* in the *roots* of your *torso*.

She is the very *heart* of the *earth,* a *damsel* who's *won* many *medals*. With a *lovely volley* of letters, she juggles a *cheap peach,* an *Argentine tangerine,* and *solemn lemons* and *melons*. At the same time, she *reaps, pares,* and then manages to *spear pears* while twirling *pastel plates* (a *staple* of her act) and balancing a *maraschino* cherry on her nose and playing two *harmonicas.*·

Pleased by what has *elapsed* and astounded by such *climaxes,* everyone *exclaims* that it would be impossible to *reproduce* her *procedure* to *intoxicate* your *excitation*. She never *mutilates* a ball, will only *stimulate ultimates*. She will not *enervate* you, and you will *venerate* her. She'll *edify* and you will *deify* the *luster* of the *result* she'll unfailingly *rustle* up.

Lucky ladies and gentlemen! *Cripes!* Just think of the *prices* we offer, as advertised in *English* on the *shingle* that adorns our booth:

DISCOUNTER INTRODUCES REDUCTIONS

Look closely at the *poster,* and *presto!*—*boing! bingo!*—you'll see an *integral alerting, altering, relating triangle*. What you see on the shingle is a trianagram—three ten-letter words, each a rearrangement of the other two! Now I, your circus pitchman, will be busy *mastering emigrants streaming* (a nine-letter trianagram) into the tent. I hope that someone will have *cautioned* them not to have *auctioned* off their *education* (yet another nine-letter trianagram). That could lead to *intercoastal altercations* (twelve-letter anagrams).

I, a *magnate gateman* who *patrols* these *portals* with your kind *permission,* have the *impression* that you brand me a *blabbing, babbling funfair ruffian,* a *has-been banshee,* a *tearing ingrate, infield infidel,* and an *errant ranter.* You may wish to *compile* a *polemic lamenting* my *alignment* as one of those *nameless salesmen* and *dishonest hedonists* who are full of *tangible bleating* and *impressing simperings.* You may claim that I who *ratchet* up the *chatter* with *supersonic percussion* am a *rowdy, wordy vice-dean* of *deviance.* You will be *eager* to *agree* that I'm a *trifling, flirting baritone obtainer* of *untidy nudity* who *seldom models* his *ideals* for *ladies.*

I may *madden* you and cause you to *demand* that I be *damned,* before you *depart,* convinced that I have *prated* and should be hoist on my own *petard, bombed* and *mobbed.* But any *outbred doubter* and *unstirred intruders* who may *obtrude* should come to the *realization* that people tend to *rationalize. Irately* and *tearily,* I tell you that, in *reality,* to be *portrayed* as one so *predatory* causes me *mental lament.* Anyone who accuses me of being a *usurping, pursuing, daemonic comedian* is simply being an *inconsistent nonscientist.*

Truth be told, I'm an *Einstein* in my *nineties—a gentleman,* an *elegant man* who gets *blamed* because I have *ambled* into *bedlam.* It's one of the *noisier ironies. However, whoever* enters needs no *caveat* to *vacate* this *auction* with *caution.* I *certify* that I will *rectify* the situation and *deposit* the *dopiest rowdies* and *weirdos* in the *closest closets.*

The *charisma* of Ana's performance *is a charm,* a *charm* that you see *march* before your eyes. In her, you *observe* the *obverse* of the very *verbose.* After the *mite* of an *item* that follows, I guarantee that at no *time* will you *emit groans* from your *organs:*

Arty Idol
Watch Ana Gram, and you will see
Her act inspires *idolatry.*
Please do not come *o tardily,*
And *dilatory* please don't be.

Adroitly Ana Gram will start
To alter *daily rot.* She's smart:
A dirty lot, an *oily dart*
She'll change into the *doily art.*

An affinity of meaning often generates an infinity of pleasure. Our arty idol Ana Gram can whirl the word *Episcopal* and create both *a Popsicle* and *Pepsi-Cola*. She tosses up a *raptor* and down swoops a *parrot*. She can even transform *dyslexia* into DAILY SEX (is that a cause or a cure?) and *antidisestablishmentarianism* into I AM AN ARTIST, AND I BLESS THIS IN ME!

But it is even more fascinating to watch Ana reconfigure words and expressions into other words or statements that bear a meaningful relationship to the base. These significant tandems are called aptagrams—words that anagram into their own synonyms or to uncannily related ideas. You clearly possess *the sense of humor* and think, "OH, THERE'S SOME FUN!" So for your entertainment I present a parade of meaningful phrase anagrams, the *athletics* of which are LITHE ACTS. Because they are so *appropriate,* they are absolutely A-I, APT, PROPER.

Ana Gram is *an acrobat*—ACT ON A BAR—as she juggles letters *alphabetically* and laughs, "I PLAY ALL THE ABC." So full of *endearments* is her magic that we bestow TENDER NAMES upon her.

You, dear *patron,* may want NO PART of me. Your *animosity* IS NO AMITY, I know. You may call me a *blatherskite* and think, "THIS BE TALKER." *Ridiculous?* I LUDICROUS. That's *asinine;* it IS INANE. So don't be *mean-spirited* and IN A DISTEMPER. Remember that *villainousness* is AN EVIL SOUL'S SIN. So *bury the hatchet* and BUTCHER THY HATE.

Now that Ana Gram is *enshrined* in your memory, I'll SEND HER IN for a GRAND FINALE—A FLARING END. After *the eyes* THEY SEE and *this ear* IT HEARS her nimble *executions,* she EXITS ON CUE, and we exclaim in *unanimity,* "AM IN UNITY!" *Mirabile dictu:* "I DUB IT A MIRACLE!"

No wonder that *anagram* is an acronym of *A New, Appropriate, Grandly Rearranged, Alphabetic Message.* No wonder that those who believe in the magical potency of words have hailed *the anagram* as AH, AN ART GEM! and *anagrams* as ARS MAGNA, "the great art"!

THE ULTIMATE ANAGRAM POEM

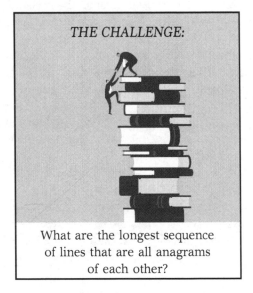

THE CHALLENGE:

What are the longest sequence
of lines that are all anagrams
of each other?

O ften, the more demanding the restrictions, the more fun I
have making a poem. I had an exhilarating time writing this
little ditty, in which each of the eleven lines is composed of
just the six letters in the name *Daniel*:

An idle
Lead-in
Ad line:
Daniel,
Nailed
In deal
(i.e., land
In dale),
Led in a
Denial
And lie.

READER CHALLENGE:

Here are seven anagrams of the
first and last names of the most
famous writer who ever set quill
to parchment. Who is he?

Has Will a peer, I ask me.
I swear he's like a lamp.
We all make his praise.
Wise male. Ah, I sparkle!
Hear me, as I will speak.
Ah, I speak a swell rime.
I am a weakish speller.

Answer
William Shakespeare.

ANAGRAM CRACKERS

In each of the following phrases, change either the first or the last word to an anagram of the other half. In each case, the anagram will be a synonym of the base word or words. For example, in the phrase "autographed the design," you would change the first word to *signed* to bring forth the ana-grammatical "signed the design." Similarly and more difficult, "Socratic word puzzle" would become "Socratic acrostic."

The first ten posers are all beastly.

1. naked bear 2. Roman goat 3. octopus excuses 4. support a lobster 5. dance-hall bearcat

6. gander peril 7. snake repents 8. crying gibbons 9. shark hears 10. silent lionesses

11. remember the cellar 12. pilot's firearm 13. viewing genies 14. hides rubies 15. most joyful epitaphs

16. resist sibling 17. entrap father 18. mother's container 19. diminutive Batman 20. resign, crooner

21. license for muteness 22. vainest residents 23. congressional treason 24. congressional rationale 25. aboard far away

26. singer's entrance 27. brides in rubble 28. hope to praise 29. married devotee 30. sees section

31. lauded diapers 32. incautious runaway 33. talented fidget 34. hurry, sleuth 35. gamester's parsley

36. Elvis survives 37. sectional shore 38. generate adolescent 39. grounded long shot 40. grandest police traps

Answers

1. bare bear 2. toga goat 3. octopus copouts 4. bolster a lobster 5. cabaret bearcat

6. gander danger 7. serpent repents 8. sobbing gibbons 9. shark harks 10. noiseless lionesses

11. recall the cellar 12. pilot's pistol 13. seeing genies 14. buries rubies 15. happiest epitaphs

16. resist sister 17. entrap parent 18. mother's thermos 19. bantam Batman 20. resign, singer

21. license for silence 22. vainest natives 23. senator treason 24. senatorial rationale 25. aboard abroad

26. singer's ingress 27. brides in debris 28. aspire to praise 29. married admirer 30. notices section

31. praised diapers 32. unwary runaway 33. gifted fidget 34. hustle, sleuth 35. player's parsley

36. Elvis lives 37. sectional coastline 38. generate teenager 39. grounded underdog 40. grandest dragnets

ON PALINDROMES

The ancient and popular Art of the Palindrome blazes out from the epicenter of the universe of letter play. Alistair Reid expresses what may be the very heart of the fascination for matters palindromic when he writes, "The dream which occupies the tortuous mind of every palindromist is that somewhere within the confines of the language lurks the Great Palindrome, the nutshell which not only fulfills the intricate demands of the art, flowing sweetly in both directions, but which also contains the Final Truth of Things." There is indeed something magic about the palindromic craft, the platonic form of making the alphabet dance.

In the quirkily brilliant *I Love Me, Vol. I,* Michael Donner explains perspicaciously that palindromania has "at last [been] correctly understood to be not a disorder at all but rather the heightened sense of order we now know it to be." To help bring order to the universe of palindromes, I offer some rubrics for creating, identifying, and ranking great palindromes.

The brevity and simplicity of single-word palindromes, such as LEVEL, REDDER, and ROTATOR, make them relatively less surprising and elegant than longer and more challenging palindromic statements. Word-unit palindromes, such as FAIR IS FOUL, AND FOUL IS FAIR; FIRST LADIES RULE THE STATE, AND STATE THE RULE— "LADIES FIRST!"; and YOU CAN CAGE A SWALLOW CAN'T YOU, BUT YOU CAN'T SWALLOW A CAGE, CAN YOU? are only a half step above. Donner observes, "Composing word-unit palindromes is an entirely different kettle of fish from composing letter-unit palindromes. . . . The word-unit composer seems to require as good a grasp of syntactic possibilities as the letter-unit composer requires of spelling possibilities. The only catch is that the two types of familiarity are quite distinct and perhaps equally hard to acquire."

Reverse whole-word reversal palindromes, such as STEP ON NO PETS, RATS LIVE ON NO EVIL STAR, and the widely circulated ABLE WAS I ERE I SAW ELBA also lack surprise. I agree with Dmitri Borgmann when he says that "almost anyone can juggle palindromic words and reversals in almost mechanical fashion until a meaningful group of words emerges. . . . [W]hat requires genuine skill is the construction of a palindromic sentence which, read in reverse, has each word sliding over from one to another into the words used in the frontward reading." The reconfiguring in the second half of the letter clusters and separating spaces in the first half of a palindromic statement contributes surprise and elegance to the adventure in letter play.

Prize palindromic statements also exhibit subject-verb structure. Cobbling a subject-verb palindromic statement is harder to pull off and, hence, more elegant when the result is successful. Moreover, subject-verb syntax inspires the reader to conjure up a clearer image of persons or things in action. IF I HAD A HI-FI; LID OFF A DAFFODIL; and even the famous A MAN! A PLAN! A CANAL! PANAMA! do not amaze the readers and conjure visions that dance in their heads as delightfully as do NURSE, I SPY GYPSIES. RUN!, SIT ON A POTATO PAN, OTIS, and STOP! MURDER US NOT, TONSURED RUMPOTS!

This matter of imagery is crucial to the greatness of a palindrome. The highest-drawer palindromic statements invoke a picture of the world that is a bubble off plumb yet somehow of our world. One *could* warn one's nurse that gypsies are nearby. Someone named Otis *could* sit on a potato pan, and shorn drunkards *could* seek to do us grave bodily harm.

Two of my favorite subject-verb palindromes are the ELK CITY, KANSAS, IS A SNAKY TICKLE and DOC, NOTE. I DISSENT. A FAST NEVER PREVENTS A FATNESS. I DIET ON COD. But as delightfully loopy as the first specimen is and as astonishing in its length and coherence as the second three-sentence jawdropper is, they do not summon vivid images to cavort in our mind's eye.

Using the rubrics of:

- elegance
- surprise
- reconfiguration of the letter clusters and spaces in the first half
- subject-verb structure, and
- bizarre imagery,

I submit that the greatest palindrome ever cobbled is GO HANG A SALAMI. I'M A LASAGNA HOG.

THE
PALINDROMEDARY

THE CHALLENGE:

How long an interview can be
constructed in which every answer
is a palindromic statement?

Ladies and gentlemen! Children of all ages! I present an exclusive interview with the Palindromedary himself, the two-way statement made flesh. This camel is a talking animal smitten with Ailihphilia— the love of palindromes. Thus, whenever the Palindromedary makes a statement, that sentence, SIDES REVERSED, IS the very same sentence.

BARKER: So you're the famous Palindromedary?

PALINDROMEDARY: I, MALE, MACHO, OH, CAMEL AM I.

I see that, despite your fame, you're wearing a name tag. Why?

GATEMAN SEES NAME. GARAGEMAN SEES NAME TAG.

Is it true that you were discovered in the Nile region?

CAMEL IN NILE, MAC.

How are you able to speak entirely in palindromes?

SPOT WORD ROW. TOPS!

What kind of word row?

WORD ROW? YA, WOW! TWO-WAY WORD ROW.

I understand that when you insert SIDES REVERSED IS into the middle of a palindrome, it becomes more than twice as long. Please offer an example.

"WORD ROW? YA, WOW! TWO-WAY WORD ROW" SIDES REVERSED IS "WORD ROW? YA, WOW! TWO-WAY WORD ROW."

Let's talk about the Word Circus animal acts. I heard that the trainer said an earful to the flying elephant in your menagerie. What was the trainer's command?

"DUMBO, LOB MUD."

I hear Dan, the lion tamer, is sick in bed and won't get up.

POOR DAN IS IN A DROOP.

Would it cheer Dan up if we dressed him in a colorful outfit?

MIRTH, SIR, A GAY ASSET? NO, DON'T ESSAY A GARISH TRIM.

So there won't be a lion performance today?

NO, SIT! CAT ACT IS ON.

Have you seen the big cats perform?

OH WHO WAS IT I SAW, OH WHO?

Well, have you seen the big cats in action?

WAS IT A CAR OR A CAT I SAW?

In addition to the big cat act, why won't we be witnessing performing dogs?

A DOG? A PANIC IN A PAGODA!

If we're not going to see a dog act, where are the dogs kept?

POOCH COOP.

I heard that somebody slipped something into the dog cage.

GOD! A RED NUGGET! A FAT EGG UNDER A DOG!

How did the dog take the prank?

HE GODDAMN MAD DOG, EH.

What happened when you followed the dog act?

DID I STEP ON DOG DOO? GOOD GOD! NO PETS! I DID!

Why aren't the owls performing tonight?

TOO HOT TO HOOT.

And the panda?

PANDA HAD NAP.

And the elk?

ELK CACKLE.

But where are the deer?

DEER FRISK, SIR, FREED.

I hear that the animals each get into a cart and have a race around the ring.

TIED, I RIDE IT.

Did you participate in the last animal race?

NO, WE NOT RACE. CART ONE WON.

The menagerie includes gnus. Did those gnus actually sing the *Star Spangled Banner?*

RISE, NUT! GNUS SUNG TUNE, SIR.

Did the rats join them?

RATS GNASH TEETH; SANG STAR.

What about the rumor that one of the gnus is ill?

UNGASTROPERITONITIS: "IS IT I? NOT I,' REPORTS A GNU.

What's the problem when you come after the gnu act?

GNU DUNG.

Will we see a yak?

KAY, A RED NUDE, PEEPED UNDER A YAK.

Is it also true that you sewed a dress for the kangaroo?

I MADE KANGAROO TUTU. TOO RAG-NAKED AM I.

What's one of your favorite human circus acts?

TRAPEZE PART.

And what's especially exciting about the trapeze?

TEN ON TRAPEZE PART! NO NET!

No net?

NO TENT NET ON.

Shall we identify and summon the acrobats to perform with the trapeze artists?

TAB OR CALL ACROBAT.

And how do the acrobats train children for their act?

PUPILS ROLL A BALL OR SLIP UP.

You seem truly excited about the circus.

AVID AS A DIVA.

Are there any acts that you would get rid of?

DUDE, NOT ONE DUD.

But what do you say to those who contend that the circus can't survive as an art form?

NO! IT CAN! ACTION!

Mr. Palindromedary, we thank you for such a scintillating two-way interview. Is it true that you are the only animal who can speak intelligibly in palindromes?

YES, THAT'S TRUE. ALL OTHER ANIMALS SAY THINGS LIKE, *"EKILS GNIH TYASS LAMINAR EHTOLLAE URTSTAHT SEY."*

PALINDROMANIA

READER CHALLENGE:

Change each phrase below to a palindrome. To create each palindrome, change one or two words in each clue to a synonym.

For example, starting with the clue "wooden crib," you would change *wooden* to *birch* to come up with the palindrome *birch crib*. Note how the *h* becomes the fulcrum, or balancing letter in the middle of such a palindrome. Sometimes you'll need such a fulcrum letter; sometimes you won't.

1. angry dam 2. speedy car 3. my workout room 4. canine god 5. maritime van

6. snoopy son 7. nurses sprint 8. mined Levi's 9. late! drat! 10. bosses weep

11. straw skin blemishes 12. personal journal raid 13. gave back diaper 14. snack containers 15. desserts under pressure

16. dog coop 17. refute a tuber 18. regal beer 19. caregivers run 20. gloomy doom

21. guru carpet 22. bold toss 23. lost sun 24. looked at decaf 25. party snare

26. amoral scent 27. shrimp warp 28. solo escorts 29. we mend 30. stinker re-stitches

31. barge robbery 32. binge on grog 33. killed rum 34. stand up, sir 35. crazy fad

36. evil martini fruit 37. experts know 38. standard cots 39. hermit's ulcer 40. some documents

41. cruel war 42. no more pots 43. annoy Sarah 44. devil breathed 45. celebrity rats

46. drab Shakespeare 47. therefore, ogre 48. lid off a flower 49. won ton? later 50. avoid Dave

Answers

1. mad dam 2. race car 3. my gym 4. dog god 5. navy van

6. nosy son 7. nurses run 8. mined denim 9. tardy! drat! 10. bosses sob

11. straw warts 12. diary raid 13. repaid diaper 14. snack cans 15. desserts stressed

16. pooch coop 17. rebut a tuber 18. regal lager 19. nurses run 20. moody doom

21. guru rug 22. bold lob 23. lost sol 24. faced decaf 25. party trap

26. amoral aroma 27. prawns warp. 28. solo gigolos 29. we sew 30. stinker reknits

31. barge grab 32. gorge grog 33. murdered rum 34. rise, sir 35. daft fad

36. evil olive 37. wonks know 38. stock cots 39. recluse's ulcer 40. some memos

41. raw war 42. stinker reknits 43. harass Sarah 44. devil lived 45. star rats

46. drab Bard 47. ergo, ogre 48. lid off a daffodil 49. won ton? not now 50. evade Dave

ATTRACTIVE
OPPOSITES

THE CHALLENGE:

How many ways can letter play
and semantics explore pairs
of words that are opposite to
each other?

O pposites attract. Opposites also attract people who love to mess around with word meanings and letters. Here's a brief logological taxonomy of fifteen yin-yanging patterns

(1) Perhaps the best-known category of opposites beyond simple antonyms, the concept of word ladders was invented by Lewis Carroll, author of *Alice in Wonderland* and *Through the Looking-Glass.* Start with a word and change one letter at each step, while keeping

the other letters in the same order, transforming the starter word ultimately into another word, often the opposite of the original. Each rung in the ladder must be a word in its own right:

HEAD	HATE	BLACK
heal	rate	blank
teal	rave	blink
tell	cave	clink
tall	cove	chink
TAIL	LOVE	chine
		whine
		WHITE

(2) **Contronyms**, pairs of words that have the same spelling and pronunciation but opposite meanings:

with. alongside; against: *a.* England fought *with* France against Germany. *b.* England fought *with* France.

out. visible; invisible: *a.* The stars are *out.* *b.* The lights are *out.*

clip. fasten; separate: *a. Clip* the coupon to the newspaper. *b. Clip* the coupon from the newspaper.

wind up. To start; to stop: *a.* It's time for me to *wind up* my watch. *b.* It's time to *wind up* this discussion.

(3) **Convergents**, two apparently opposite words or expressions that have the same meaning:

Loosen and *unloosen* mean the same thing.

A *good licking* and a *bad licking* are the same thing.

A *slim chance* and a *fat chance* are the same thing.

Your alarm clock goes *off* and *on* at the same time.

(4) **Rhyming antonyms**, rhyming words that are opposite of each other:

adore / abhor   glad / sad   hired / fired

(5) **Antigrams**, anagrammed words or phrases that communicate opposite meanings:

words:

united / untied   ruthful / hurtful   marital / martial

(Some might interpret that last pairing as synonymous.)

words and phrases:

antagonist / not against   filled / ill-fed   funeral / real fun

(6) **Anticharades,** words that when cleft into two or more parts, reveal their own opposites:

amok / am o.k.   inaction / in action   therapist / the rapist

(7) **Punctuational opposites,** statements that convey opposite meanings when their punctuation is altered:

Woman: without her, man is helpless. / Woman without her man is helpless.

I would like to tell you that I love you. I can't stop thinking that you are one of the prettiest women on earth. /

I would like to tell you that I love you. I can't. Stop thinking that you are one of the prettiest women on earth.

(8) **Beheaded opposites,** words that, when their first letter is lopped off, become their own opposites:

bonus / onus   covert / overt   preview / review

(9) **Antiroos** (another term I've neologized), kangaroo words that, when some letters are deleted, retain the original order of the remaining letters and become their own opposites:

courteous / curt   saintliness / sin   threat / treat

(10) **Letter substitution opposites,** wherein the replacement of a letter by another letter begets an opposite:

auspicious / suspicious   collision / collusion   milestone / millstone

We can imagine other possible contrastive clusters that may tremble into birth if readers can supply authentic examples:

(11) **Curtailment opposites,** words that, when their last letters are lopped off, become their own opposites. *Infinitesimal/infinite* is a lovely example of multiple curtailment, but single-letter curtailments beyond the drab categories of plural-singular *words-word, female-male,* and *fiancée/fiancé* appear to be in short or no supply.

(12) **Homophonic antonyms,** two words that sound the same, are spelled differently, and have opposite meanings. There appears to be only one authentic pairing: *raise/raze.* Other attempts, such as *reckless/wreckless,* are contrived.

FORTUNATE
REVERSALS

THE CHALLENGE:

How many words form new words
by simply switching their halves?

We loony logologists love to switch around letters within words—adjacent letters (*united-untied*), separated letters (*conversation-conservation*), and initial and terminal letters (*latches-satchel*). In some words we can interchange each half to form new words. I call these leapfrogging specimens "fortunate reversals."

At least two letters must vault from front word to back word. Thus, single-letter looping anagrams are excluded, such as (I'm sticking to just animals here) *ant-tan, asp-spa, drake-raked, emus muse, ewe-wee, flea-leaf, manatee-emanate* (magnificent!), *mite-emit, owl-low, rhea-hear, shark-harks, snail-nails,* and *swine-wines.*

Also outlawed are reversible compounds, such as *birdsong-song-bird, bookcase-casebook, gunshot-shotgun, horserace-racehorse, jayvee-veejay,* and even *Tokyo-Kyoto* (a reversal of two morphemes that mean "capital city"). That's because the soul of logology is letter play, not morphemic manipulation; alphabetic accidents, not the syntactic rearrangement of meaning-bearing elements. That's also why I bar particle verbs, such as *holdup-uphold, outtake-takeout,* and *setup-upset,* and reduplications and other double-identity words, such as *bonbon, dodo, hotshots, meme, murmur, muumuu,* and *testes.*

But if an interchange of morphemes (meaning-bearing elements) creates two new morphemes, the fraternal twins qualify as bona fide fortunate reversals. The likes of *allocation-locational, bloodshot-hot bloods, headshot-hotheads,* and *ownership-shipowner* do not pass muster because, in each switcheroo, one morpheme changes, and one stays the same. But if two transposed morphemes metamorphose into two new morphemes, as in the two eight-letter examples at the end of this disquisition, they gain an honored seat in the pantheon.

Each reversal must be written as a single word. Hence, *mango-go man, callow-low-cal, hatred-red hat, Fargo-go far, prosecute-cute prose, potshot-hot pots, tactic Tic Tac,* and *potshots-hot spots* are denied entry.

As has been my practice over the decades, I minimize arcane words, such as *ancle-clean, balsa-sabal,* and *dozen-zendo.* I also include common names of people, places, and things but exclude uncommon spellings, such as in *Betti Tibet, Cherlyn lyncher, Coreen encore, Derwin winder, Gerti tiger, Herma Maher, Kerma maker, Kerwin winker, Kylea leaky,* and *Mena name,*

On the other hand, I do include other proper nouns, such as *Lyon-only;* free-standing roots, such as *game-mega;* and the British spelling *-re,* such as *centre-recent.*

Now cast your eyes upon one hundred and fifty four-to-eight-letter, imposing, transposing, swapping, flip-flopping, rotating, relocating, reciprocating fortunate reversals:

4 letters

Alan anal	chin inch	Eric icer	loos Oslo
Amex exam	chit itch	Erma Maer	Lyon only
ankh Khan	Chou ouch	fire refi	lyre rely
Anna naan	code deco	game mega	mesa same
anon Onan	dale Leda	gaol Olga	meta tame
arch char	Dana nada	gave Vega	Neva vane
arse sear	demo mode	Ilsa sail	Otto toot
arts tsar	Desi side	isle leis	pore repo
Boca Cabo	dyed eddy	Kira raki	pyro ropy
boho hobo	else seel	kiwi wiki	rave Vera
bolo lobo	emit item	lima Mali	rite Teri
Cain Inca	ergo goer	Levi vile	Ruth thru

5 letters

admen menad	bowel elbow	karma Makar
alloy loyal	braze zebra	Lamar Marla
Alton tonal	Costa tacos	Laver Verla
angle glean	crone necro	lever Verle
angst Stang	danse sedan	Lonny nylon
arced cedar	Dylan Landy	Lyman manly
Arden denar	Edwin wined	Lysol Solly
arson sonar	estop topes	manor Norma
aside ideas	hadji jihad	Marta Tamar
aspic picas	Hamas Masha	mense semen
astro roast	intra train	mitre remit
boles lesbo	Jason Sonja	never Verne

onset Seton	Petri tripe	saver versa
pasta tapas	raise serai	Serta taser
paves Vespa	rater terra	sever verse
Pedro roped	rinse serin	slate Tesla
pesky Skype	route utero	state testa
pesto stope	rusty Tyrus	stave vesta
pesty types	sates Tessa	Tavis vista

In the above lineup, we observe some semantic relationships within *bowel-elbow*, *hadji-jihad*, and *pasta-tapas*.

One four-step example stands atop this five-letter cluster: *Pesto* yields *stope* and *topes*, and *topes* yields *estop*.

6 letters

abacas casaba	enamor morena	ingrow rowing
ablest stable	enlist listen	insole oleins
alpine pineal	Ernest nester	lysing singly
altars tarsal	errant ranter	mother thermo
ascent centas	erring ringer	Nassau saunas
bedlam lambed	German manger	nester Sterne
Berger Gerber	geyser Sergey	perves vesper
centre recent	harlot Lothar	ranter terran
dentin indent	iatric Tricia	ripest stripe
Edward warded	Ingrid riding	selves vessel

Gleaming out from the six-letter reversals, *Sterne* yields *Ernest*, which in turn yields *nester*; and *errant* yields *ranter*, which in turn yields *terran*, which, as every sci-fi fan knows, means "earth dweller."

7 letters

asquint quintas	kingpin pinking
ingrain raining	Lessing singles
inspect pectins	questor torques
Kerstin stinker	redrive rivered
Kerstin tinkers	respect spectre

Within this sesquipedalian cluster, we do find one triple play: *tinkers* yields *Kerstin,* which in turn yields *stinker.*

8 letters

barstool toolbars	mentally tallymen

While it could be argued that *barstool* and *toolbars* share the same morpheme, *bar,* the credentials for *mentally-tallymen* appear to be impeccable.

THE HOLY GRAIL OF LETTER PLAY

THE CHALLENGE:

What word exhibits the
greatest number of intriguing
logological features?

S ome words are beguiling, bedazzling, and bewitching because
their letters exhibit a strikingly unique property. This is the
world of logology.

Take the word *ambidextrous*. Digging up the roots of *ambidextrous*, an etymologist discovers that the word is a composite of two Latin roots, *ambi* and *dexter*, that mean "using both the left and right hands with equal ease."

A logologist, on the other hand, is fascinated by letter patterns and, hence, beguiled by the fact that *ambidextrous* is alphabetically ambidextrous. Its left half, *ambide,* uses letters only from the left half of the alphabet, and its right half, *xtrous,* uses letters only from the right half of the alphabet. Add an *–ly,* and you get a fourteen-letter isogram—*ambidextrously*—a word in which no letter is repeated. That's just one letter short of the fifteen-letter isogrammatical champion, *uncopyrightable.*

Here, alphabetically, are more of my favorite logological wonders:

- *Blossom* is a seven-letter noun and verb with a double letter in the middle. Pluck that double letter, and you end up with the five-letter word *bloom,* with a different double letter in the middle, but with the same meaning as *blossom* as a noun and as a verb.

- *Bookkeeper* is the only common word that features three consecutive pairs of double letters. It is easy to imagine the bookkeeper's assistant, a *subbookkeeper,* who boasts four consecutive pairs of double letters.

  Now let's conjure up a zoologist who helps maintain raccoon habitats. We'd call that zoologist a *raccoon nook keeper*—six consecutive sets of double letters!

  Not done: Now let's imagine another zoologist who studies the liquid inside chickadee eggs. We'd call this scientist a *chickadee egg goo-ologist*—and into the world is born three consecutive sets of triple letters!

- *Facetious* is the shortest (nine letters) and most accessible word that contains all five major vowels—*a, e, i, o,* and *u*—in alphabetical order.

- How many letters are there in the state name *Mississippi*? Eleven, of course—but one could also say four—*m, i, s,* and *p.* In letter patterning, *Mississippi* is clearly the best of the state names, rivaled only by *Tennessee.* Both names contain just one vowel repeated four times, three sets of double letters, and only four different letters.

  But *Mississippi* has the distinction of containing a seven-letter embedded palindrome—*issississi;* three sequential four-letter palindromes—*issi, issi,* and *ippi;* and a double triple—*ississ.*

And each year is crowned a new *Miss Mississippi,* whose title consists of three double triples—*Missmiss, ississ,* and *ssissi.*

- *Nth,* as in "to the nth degree," is the only common English word that doesn't contain any vowel—*a, e, i, o, u,* y, or *w.*

- A *pastern* is the part of a horse's foot between the fetlock and the top of the hoof.

   Logologically *pastern* is the most chardeable of all words in the English language. That is, when you sextuply cleave *pastern* at any point in the word, you will come up with two words.

   As you look at the changing two halves, bear in mind that all letters are entries in dictionaries and hence qualify as words, that *ern* is a variant spelling for a long-winged species of sea eagle, that a *paster* is someone who pastes, and that an *RN* is a registered nurse:

   p astern pa stern pas tern past ern paste RN paster n

- *Pneumonoultramicroscopicsilicovolcanoconiosis* is the most capacious, hippopotomonstrosesquipedalian word enshrined in *Merriam Webster's Third New International Dictionary* and, since 1982, the longest in the *Oxford English Dictionary.* The word describes a miners' disease caused by inhaling too much quartz or silicate dust. Among its forty-five letters and nineteen syllables occur nine *o*'s, surely the record for a letter most repeated within a single word; six *c*'s; and but one *e.*

- *Queue* is the only word that can have its last four letters curtailed and still retain its original pronunciation. *Queueing* is also the only common word in English that houses five consecutive vowels.

- *Strengths* is one of a number of nine-letter words of one syllable and the longest containing but a single vowel. Among its strengths is the fact that it ends with five consecutive consonants.

- *Temperamentally* is the densest example of a snowball word, one that can be cleft into one-, two-, three-, four-, and five-letter words: *t em per amen tally.*

- *TWENTY-NINE* is spelled with letters made of straight lines only—29 of them!

- *A zyzzyva* is a genus of tropical South American snouted weevil discovered in Brazil. No longer than an ant, this insect could be labeled "the lesser of two weevils."

  With the first five of its seven letters being *z* or *y*, *zyzzyva* is the last word in many dictionaries.

All words, no matter how common or obscure, are interesting, but some are more interesting than others. And out of the some, a few are interesting in more than one way. And out of the few, one word is more interesting in more ways than any other word in the English language. It is packed with properties that range from common to unique. It stands out from the outstanding. What is that word? The quest to find it is the ultimate exercise in letterplay—the search for the Logological Holy Grail, the best of all possible words.

Over the course of a series of e-missives, fellow recreational linguist Dave Morice and I noticed something, then many things, about the word PEPPERTREE, defined as "a Peruvian evergreen tree (*Schinus molle*) of the cashew family grown as a shade tree in mild regions." As words go, PEPPERTREE is neither common nor obscure. It's easy enough to get a general idea of what it means.

First of all, logologically speaking, PEPPERTREE is a ten-letter pyramid word, one that contains one occurrence of one letter, two of another, three of a third, and four of a fourth:

T

RR

PPP

EEEE

This pattern occurs in only a few other words of that length, including SLEEVELESS and TENNESSEE'S. For that reason alone, PEPPERTREE is remarkable.

This chapter lists more than twenty ways in which PEPPERTREE does something unusual in its letters and pronunciation:

- PEPPERTREE is a ten-letter word that can be typed using only the letters on the *qwerty* row of a standard keyboard. The others are *pepperroot, pepperwort, perpetuity, proprietor, repertoire,* and—ta da!—*typewriter.*

- Without its first letter, (P)EPPERTREE can be divided into two strings of letters, EPP and ERTREE, both of which form pyramids. Together, EPP, ERTREE, and PEPPERTREE form a triple pyramid, but in this case the smaller pyramids are letter strings that don't overlap instead of words, PEP and PEPPER, that do.

- If prefixes are allowed, then PEPPERTREE is not only a pyramid word, but also a snowball word: P EP PER TREE. (EP appears in the *Oxford English Dictionary* as a shortened form of EPI.)

- Without its last letter, PEPPERTRE(E) can be divided into three overlapping palindromes—PEP, EPPE, and ERTRE. They have increasing lengths of three, four, and five letters. Two letters overlap between the first two palindromes, and one letter between the last two.

- Without its first letter, (P)EPPERTREE can be divided into three palindromes—EPPE, RTR, and EE. They have decreasing lengths of four, three, and two letters. No letters overlap, and no letters fall between them.

- Its consonants occur in clusters, each separated by the vowel E, that form the most basic arithmetic progression—1, 2, and 3 (P, PP, RTR).

- All the letters in PEPPERTREE stand on vertical lines.

- Half of its letters have curves, and half don't: PPPRR (occurring in alphabetic order), EETEE (occurring in palindromic order).

- Half of its letters have closed spaces, and half don't: PPPRR, EETEE.

- In lowercase, each letter in *peppertree* is composed of one line and one curve.

- In lowercase, half of its letters have vertical lines and half have horizontal lines: ppprr, eetee.

- In its three syllables, PEPPERTREE contains three soundings of the letter E—short, schwa, and long.

- PEPPERTREE is an EVERGREEN, and each of these two words is a univocalic using the letter E four times.

- E, the most commonly occurring letter in PEPPERTREE, is the only letter of the alphabet with three horizontal lines. Just as E's lone vertical line supports its three horizontal lines, so the vowel E supports the three different consonants, PRT, in the word's three syllables.

- E appears the most (four times), and T appears the least (one time). The alphabetic value (A=1, B=2, etc.) of E is 5. Adding the values of the 4 E's gives 5 + 5 + 5 + 5 = 20, which is the alphabetic value of T.

- Its single vowel, E, reposes in the first half of the alphabet, and its consonants, P, R, and T, occupy in the second half.

- Its vowels occupy odd-numbered positions in the alphabet, and its consonants occupy even-numbered positions.

- Listing each of the four different letters in order of first appearance in PEPPERTREE spells PERT, which describes the logological characteristics of PEPPERTREE itself.

- Similarly, the longest string of different letters in PEPPERTREE appears in the very center and spells PERT.

- Arranging all the letters of PEPPERTREE in order of number of occurrences, from greatest to least, results in EEEE PPP RR T. Alphabetizing all the letters results in the exact same arrangement.

- The letter P looks like a leaf. When the P's fall off the PEPPERTREE, the remaining letters form a palindrome, EERTREE, in which the T stands like a tree among the letters that branch out to spell TREE in both directions.

BODY LANGUAGE

I t's fun to look at categories of words for their letter patterns.

READER CHALLENGE:

Identify the letter pattern that
unites each of the following
five-animal clusters:

- deer, dog, gnat, ram, rat;
- category, crowned, dogma, emulate, wrench;
- blotter, escrow, forebear, scallion, vamoose;
- ant, asp, manatee, mite, owl.

In the first list, each word becomes another word when spelled backwards. In the second, each word begins with the name of an animal. In the third, each word ends with an animal. In the fourth, each beastly word becomes a new word when its last letter is looped to the front of the word.

Now let's turn to body language:

Whether you're a highbrow or lowbrow, here's some jaw-dropping, knee-slapping, rib-tickling fun you can really sink your teeth into. Try your hand at getting a leg up on some head-to-toe body English. I'm not speaking tongue-in-cheek when I say that, as a rule of thumb, all answers pertain to easily recognizable body parts.

1. Let's start with some simple anatomy. Name at least ten parts of the body that are each spelled with just three letters.

2. What do the following definitions have in common: last part of some books, architectural support, young bovine, prison dwelling, storage container? Once you ascertain the pattern, come up with at least dozen more examples.

3. What do these homophonic words have in common: *hare, hart,* and *heal?* Once you ascertain the pattern, come up with a dozen more.

4. What do these anagramable words have in common: *are, barest, below,* and *booms?* Once you ascertain the pattern, come up with thirty more.

5. Identify one palindromic body part.

6. What two parts of the body become plural by changing their internal vowels, in the manner of *man-men?*

7. With three different letters tacked onto the front, the word *arm* becomes *farm, harm,* and *warm.* What other three-letter body part can be preceded by thirteen different letters to form thirteen different words?

8. Identify a part of the body that consists of six letters and in which the first three letters repeat themselves in order.

9. Identify an internal organ that consists of ten letters, including all six in the previous answer. The first five letters of this word also repose in the second half but in a different order.

10. I'm sure I won't leave you red-faced if I ask you to list as many colorful body expressions as you can (i.e. body parts joined with colors).

Answers

1. arm, ear, eye, gum, gut, hip, jaw, lap, leg, lid, lip, rib, toe

2. Each yields a word that is also a part of the body: appendix, arch, calf, cell, and chest or trunk. Additional examples include colon, gum, head, hip, iris, joint, lap, lash, limb, mole, nail, organ, palm, pupil, sole, temple.

3. Each is a homophone of a body part. Additional examples include I / aye, browse, knows, limn, mussel, navel, nee, palette / pallet, poor / pour, scull, soul, toe, vane / vain, waste.

4. Each is an anagram of a body part. Additional examples include bowel-elbow, bread-beard, cafe-face, char-arch, clasp-scalp, done-node, earth-heart, eons-nose, fringe-finger, gel-leg, groan-organ, inch-chin, sink-skin, keen-knee, lain-nail, lamp-palm, limped-dimple, lose-sole, mug-gum, pane-nape, ram-arm, rope-pore, roost-roots, shelf-flesh, stub-bust, wines-sinew, suture-uterus, tape-pate, tsetse-testes, tug-gut, venal-navel, viler-liver, waits-waist, writs-wrist.

5. eye, boob, tit

6. foot-feet, tooth-teeth

7. ear: bear, dear, fear, gear, hear, Lear, near, pear, rear, sear, tear, wear, year

8. testes

9. intestines

10. black eye, blackface, Blackbeard, Blackfoot, blackhead, black-hearted, black thumb, blue balls, Bluebeard, blueblood, blue hair, bluenose, brown-nose, Goldfinger, Goldilocks; green-eyed, green thumb; greybeard, lily-livered, pink eye, Purple Heart, red-blooded, red-breast, red-eye, red-faced, red-handed, redhead, redneck, red nose, redskin, silver-tongued, whitehead, white knuckles, yellow-bellied.

THE DANCING
ALPHABET

READER CHALLENGE:

Within each five-word set that
follows lurks a common denominator, a characteristic shared by every
word in the cluster. All the answers,
which follow the quiz, relate to the
letter patterns in each cluster. For
example, in the words *catchphrase,
latchstring,* and *weltschmerz*
appear six consonants in a row.
For another example,
ambidextrously, dermatoglyphics,
and *uncopyrightable* are long words
within which no letter is repeated.

Typical of this kind of challenge, some of the lists will stump you the first time around. But insights will come to you in sudden flashes as you return to the game a second or third time.

1. parse, pears, reaps, spare, spear

2. deified, noon, pep, redder, sees

3. dissident, hosannas, millimeter, sniffing, suffuse

4. calmness, hijack, indefinite, stuck, worst

5. dialogue, equation, facetious, housemaid, sequoia

6. gypsy, myrrh, nth, pygmy, rhythms

7. giggling, maharaja, possess, razzmatazz, whippersnapper

8. bassoon, coffee, raccoon, roommate, tattoo

9. abhors, almost, begins, biopsy, chintz

10. barbaric, bringing, counterterrorism, possessed, ratcatcher

11. banana, cocoon, horror, mammal, tattoo

12. civic, civil, livid, mimic, vivid

13. selective, sexist, slake, stern, swindles

14. frightful, president, revolution, treason, vindicate

15. caress, hearth, honest, needless, ration

16. Jackson, Hayes, Hoover, Nixon, Washington

17. banana, grammar, petite, redivide, revere

18. eight, neither, science, sovereign, weird

19. area, aria, idea, iota, oleo

20. are, came, gape, lien, rode

Answers

1. All these words are anagrams of each other. 2. palindromes, which read the same forward and backward 3. words containing double letters, but, to be more elegant, words in which is embedded a six-letter palindrome 4. words that contain three letters in adjacent alphabetical order 5. words that include all of the major vowels—*a, e, i, o,* and *u*

6. words bereft of any of the major vowels 7. words that contain four instances of one letter 8. words with two touching sets of double letters 9. letters appear in alphabetical order 10. words featuring adjacent pairs of triple letters

11. pyramid words, in which a letter occurs once, a second letter twice, and a third letter three times 12. words that, when capitalized, consist entirely of Roman numerals

13. words that become new words when the initial *s* is looped to the back 14. words that become new words when the first letter is deleted 15. words that become new words when the last letter is deleted

16. presidents' last names that are each composed of two words 17. words that spell themselves backwards when the first letter is looped to the back of the word 18. words that violate the "*i* before *e,* except after *c*" rule 18. words that contain all of the major vowels 19. three-syllable words with just one consonant 20. words that change from one syllable to three when a letter is added to the front or the back—*area, cameo, agape, alien, rodeo*

LETTERS ARE
FOREVER

hat better way to end a cluster of letter-perfect chapters than with a letter-perfect quiz?

READER CHALLENGE:

In each list that follows, a parade
of letters marches in alphabetical
order. What do the letters
in each line have in common?

The letters within each of the following lineups share a commonality of sound:

1. ABCGIJKLMNOPQRTUXY

2. BCDEGPTVZ

3. AJK

4. QUW

5. FHLMNORSX

What aspect of design accounts for the unity in each of the following clusters?:

6. AEFHIKLMNTVWXYZ

7. BCDGJOPQRSU

8. AHIMOTUVWXY

9. BCDEHUKOX

10. HINOSXZ

Finally, what concept other than sound or shape unites each of the following letter strings?:

11. BCDFGHJKLMNPQRSTVXZ

12. CDILMVX

13. AJKQ

14. EIOPQRTUWY

15. ADEHILNORSTU

Answers
1. Each letter sounds the same as a full word. 2. 3. 4. When all the letters are sounded, they rhyme. 5. These letters do not rhyme with any other letters.

6. Each letter is built from straight lines. 7. Each letter contains one or more curved lines. 8. Each letter exhibits vertical symmetry; its left and right sides are mirror images. 9. Each letter exhibits horizontal symmetry; its top and bottom are mirror images. 10. Each letter remains the same when turned upside down.

11. Each letter is a consonant. I exclude y and *w* because they sometimes act as vowels. 12. Each letter is a Roman numeral. 13. Each letter appears on playing cards. 14. These letters repose on the top row of letters on a standard *qwerty* keyboard. 15. These twelve letters appear the most frequently in print. Frequency lists vary, but a typical lineup gives the order as ETAOINSHRDLU.

THE GLAMOUR
OF GRAMMAR

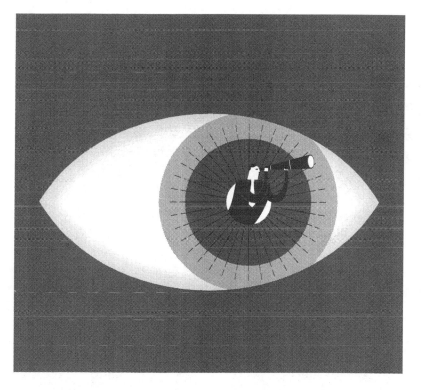

FAMILIARITY
BREEDS CONFUSION

Believe it or not, *grammar* and *glamour* are historically the same word. Back in the eighteenth century one of the meanings of *grammar* was "magic, enchantment." The Scots let the *r* slip into an *l,* and lo, came forth *glamour.* In the popular mind, however, grammar is anything but glamorous. Whatever magic resides in the subject is felt to be a sort of black magic, a mysterious caldron bubbling with creepy, crawly creatures. In this, the third neighborhood of *Challenging Words for Smart People,* I hope to make the study of grammar an intellectual blast for you, my perspicacious reader.

Two central elements of grammar are word choice and structure. The first two chapters of this cluster will focus on word choice, the rest on how words go to work structurally.

READER CHALLENGE:

Here's a game
to whet your appetite—
or (great expectorations!)
is it wet your appetite?—
for troublesome twins and triplets
living in our English language.

The phrases below may be as familiar to you as your old stamping—or is it stomping?—grounds, but when it comes to spelling them, you may be in dire straights—or is it dire straits? Like the cat that ate cheese and then breathed into the mouse hole, I'm sure that you're waiting with baited—or should that be bated?—breath and chomping (or perhaps champing?) at the bit. May your answers and mine jibe—or maybe jive?—completely so that you don't miss any by a hare's breath—or hare's breadth? or hair's breath? or hair's breadth?

Homophones and soundalikes can often reck—or is it wreck or wreak?—havoc. In each phrase that follows, choose the preferred spelling.

1. anchors *away/aweigh* 2. to wait with *baited/bated* breath 3. to grin and *bare/bear* it 4. sound *bite/byte* 5. *bloc/block* voting

6. a *ceded/seeded* player 7. *champing/chomping* at the bit 8. a full *complement/compliment* of 9. to strike a responsive *chord/cord* 10. just *deserts/desserts*

11. doesn't *faze/phase* me 12. to have a *flair/flare* for 13. *foul/fowl* weather 14. *hail/hale* and *hardy/hearty* 15. a *hair's/hare's breadth/breath*

16. a seamless *hole/whole* 17. a friend in need is a friend *in deed/ indeed* 18. it doesn't *jibe/jive* 19. on the *lam/lamb* 20. to the *manner/ manor born/borne*

21. *marshal/martial* law 22. to test one's *medal/meddle/metal/ mettle* 23. *might/mite* and *mane/main* 24. beyond the *pale/pail* 25. to *peak/peek/pique* one's interest

26. *pi/pie* in the sky 27. *pidgin/pigeon* English 28. *plain/plane* geometry 29. to *pore/pour* over an article 30. *praying/preying* mantis

31. a matter of *principal/ principle* 32. *rack/wrack* one's brain 33. to give free *rain/reign/rein* 34. *raise/raze Cain/cane* 35. to pay *rapped/rapt/wrapped* attention

36. with *reckless/wreckless* abandon 37. to *reek/wreak/wreck* havoc 38. *right/rite/write* of passage 39. a *shoe-/shoo-*in 40. to *sic/sick* the dog on someone

41. *sleight/slight* of hand 42. *spit and/spitting* image 43. the old *stamping/stomping* grounds 44. to *stanch/staunch* the flow 45. dire *straights/straits*

46. a *toe-/tow-headed* youth 47. to *toe/tow* the line 48. a real *trooper/trouper.* 49. all in *vain/vane/vein* 50. to *wet/whet* one's appetite

Answers
1. aweigh 2. bated 3. bear 4. bite 5. bloc 6. seeded 7. champing or chomping 8. complement 9. chord 10. deserts
11. faze 12. flair 13. foul 14. hale/hearty 15. hair's breadth 16. whole 17. indeed 18. jibe 19. lam 20. manner born
21. martial 22. mettle 23. might/main 24. pale 25. pique 26. pie 27. pidgin 28. plane 29. pore 30. praying
31. principle 32. rack 33. rein 34. raise Cain 35. rapt 36. reckless 37. wreak 38. rite 39. shoo- 40. sic
41. sleight 42. spitting 43. stamping 44. stanch 45. straits 46. tow 47. toe 48. trouper 49. vain 50. whet

THE DIFFERENCE
A WORD MAKES

Which dog has the upper paw?:

a. A clever dog knows its master.
b. A clever dog knows it's master.

The answer is the dog in the second sentence because that dog knows that it is master.

READER CHALLENGE:

To discover how a slight difference in wording and (toward the end) punctuation can make a vast difference in meaning, examine each pair of sentences and choose the one that answers the question correctly:

1. Which baseball player has wings?

    a. The batter flew out to left field.

    b. The batter flied out to left field.

2. Which judge would you prefer?

    a. At the trial, the judge was completely uninterested.

    b. At the trial, the judge was completely disinterested.

3. Which students received a special exemption?

    a. The draft board excepted all students.

    b. The draft board accepted all students.

4. Which pair had met previously?

    a. We were formally introduced.

    b. We were formerly introduced.

5. Which Pat is a girl?

    a. Pat was smarter than the boys in the class.

    b. Pat was smarter than the other boys in the class.

6. Which request would parents more likely make to their children?

    a. Bring the stray dog home.

    b. Take the stray dog home.

7. Which runner put her foot down?

    a. She hoped to reach the finish line.

    b. She hopped to reach the finish line.

8. Which dog is definitely not a bloodhound?

    a. The dog smelled badly.

    b. The dog smelled bad.

9. Which Hood was careless?

    a. In tense situations, Robin Hood would loose arrows.

    b. In tense situations, Robin Hood would lose arrows.

10. Which newspapers are dishonest?

    a. The newspapers lied about the casino's sports book.
    b. The newspapers lay about the casino's sports book.

11. Which camper can see the sky?

    a. The camper lay prone on the grass.
    b. The camper lay supine on the grass.

12. Which child sticks out like a sore thumb in a crowd?

    a. Mother went shopping with her tow-headed son.
    b. Mother went shopping with her toe-headed son.

13. Which caveman liked the company of others?

    a. Ug found a club.
    b. Ug founded a club.

14. Which John is a thespian?

    a. John acted as an old man.
    b. John acted like an old man.

15. Which speaker is smarter?

    a. In the room were four geniuses beside me.
    b. In the room were four geniuses besides me.

16. Which twosome is playing doubles?

    a. Juliet complemented Romeo's tennis game.
    b. Juliet complimented Romeo's tennis game.

17. Which is the greater compliment?

    a. I know you're superior.
    b. I know your superior.

18. Which leader is more resourceful?

    a. The mayor adapted her predecessor's policies.
    b. The mayor adopted her predecessor's policies.

19. Which town boasts strong educational leadership?

    a. I admire the town's principles.
    b. I admire the town's principals.

20. Which student will earn the higher grade?

    a. His answers were all most accurate.
    b. His answers were almost accurate.

21. In which case is Percy cashing in on his father's power?

    a. Percy flaunts his father's authority.
    b. Percy flouts his father's authority.

22. Which person is more skeptical?

    a. She is an incredible reader.
    b. She is an incredulous reader.

23. Which invitation is more dangerous?

    a. I invite you to desert.
    b. I invite you to dessert.

24. Which structure got bombed?

    a. The soldiers raised the fort.
    b. The soldiers razed the fort.

25. In which statement can you put a sock?

    a. It's darned good.
    b. It's darned well.

26. Which marriage is stronger?

    a. My wife likes golf better than I.
    b. My wife likes golf better than me.

27. Which man could be called a Romeo?

    a. He spent a lot of time repelling women.
    b. He spent a lot of time repulsing women.

28. Which woman is a magician?

    a. She embellished her talk with a series of allusions.
    b. She embellished her talk with a series of illusions.

29. In which situation should you be careful about lighting a match?

    a. In the room stood a tank of inflammable gas.
    b. In the room stood a tank of nonflammable gas.

30. Which nation is safer?

    a. Our country has the ultimate defense system.
    b. Our country has the penultimate defense system.

31. Which person was not invited to the party?

    a. They left me out of the party.
    b. They let me out of the party.

32. Which car is worth more?

    a. The car is of infinite value.
    b. The car is of infinitesimal value.

33. Which statement definitely includes two people?

    a. Mary inferred that she was unhappy with the job.
    b. Mary implied that she was unhappy with the job.

34. Which airplane poses the greater danger?

    a. The plane will be in the air soon.
    b. The plane will be in the air momentarily.

35. Which company is in more trouble?

    a. The company is floundering.
    b. The company is foundering.

36. Which employee should be fired?

    a. The butler stood at the door and called the guests names.
    b. The butler stood at the door and called the guests' names.

37. Which situation is worse for the Democratic party?

    a. Democrats who are seen as weak will not be elected.

    b. Democrats, who are seen as weak, will not be elected.

38. Which scene is more threatening?

    a. I saw a man eating lobster.

    b. I saw a man-eating lobster.

39. Which speaker is Ishmael's girlfriend?

    a. Call me Ishmael.

    b. Call me, Ishmael.

40. Which speaker is a cannibal?

    a. Let's eat, Grandma.

    b. Let's eat Grandma.

Answers

a 2. b 3. a 4. b 5. a 6. b 7. b 8. a 9. b 10. a

11. b 12. b 13. b 14. a 15. b 16. a 17. a 18. a 19. b 20. a

21. a 22. b 23. a 24. b 25. b 26. a 27. a 28. b 29. a 30. a

31. a 32. a 33. a 34. b 35. b 36. a 37. b 38. b 39. b 40. b

CONVERTIBLE ENGLISH

THE CHALLENGE:

How versatilely can words convert
from one part of speech to another?

Because modern English has shed most of the flexional endings
that distinguish grammatical functions, many of our words
possess the lively ability to rail-jump from one part of speech
to another without any basic change in form. This happy facility,
variously called conversion or function shift, endows our vocabulary
with vitality, power, and a prolific source of new words.

Without being fully aware of it, many of us cut our punning eye
teeth on riddles that are built on function shift:

- What has four wheels and flies?
  A garbage truck.
- What makes the Tower of Pisa lean?
  It never eats.
- Why did Silly Billy blush when he opened the refrigerator?
  He saw the salad dressing.
- Why didn't Silly Billy complete his cross-country trip?
  Every time he saw a "Clean Rest Rooms" sign, he went in and cleaned them.
- Have you ever seen a home run, a ski jump, and a salad bowl?

Even standard sentences can bounce a reader back and forth from one meaning to another:
- Time flies like an arrow. Fruit flies like a banana.
- The detective looked hard.
- Pam hated visiting relatives.
- I know you like the palm of my hand.
- Headline: RAIN CLOUDS WELCOME AT AIRPORT
- I know a man with a feebly growing down upon his chin.

The most common variety of function shift is the transfer of a word established as a noun into a verb. As is the case with babies learning to speak, so it is with the history of language. First comes a concept; then comes an action. Consider the names we give to parts of the body. Almost any of these, without much ado or ceremony, can convert to a verb. We *head* a committee, *eye* a job opportunity, *face* a problem, *shoulder* a load, *elbow* our way through a crowd, *foot* a bill, or *toe* the line—without any modification in the form of each word. Here are forty anatonyms, as they are called—verbalized body parts:

arm	elbow	gut	knuckle	scalp
back	eye	hand	lip	shoulder
belly	face	head	mouth	skin
body	finger	heel	muscle	stomach
bone	fist	hip	neck	thumb
brain	flesh	jaw	nose	toe
breast	foot	knee	palm	tongue
chin	gum	kneecap	rib	wrist

Similarly, we can *chicken* out, *clam* up, *ram* a car, and *wolf* our food. From a menagerie of animal names, we can exhibit at least fifty such noun-into-verb specimens:

ape	chicken	ferret	horse	rook
badger	clam	fish	hound	skunk
birdie	cow	flounder	louse	snake
bird dog	crab	fox	monkey	snipe
bitch	crane	frog	parrot	sponge
buck	crow	goose	pig	squirrel
buffalo	dog	grouse	pony	toad
bug	duck	gull	quail	weasel
bull	eagle	hawk	ram	wolf
carp	fawn	hog	rat	worm

An especially intriguing category of noun-into-verb conversion, sometimes known as Phyfe's Rule, involves a shift of stress from the front of the noun to the back of the verb, often accompanied by a change in the sound of a vowel.

The person who wrote the following ad apparently hadn't mastered the subtleties of this pattern: "Unmarried women wanted to pick fruit and produce at night."

Similarly, on the side of my recycling bin is emblazoned:

City of San Diego
Environmental Services
Refuse Collection

What a waste of recyclables!

Most, but not all, of these words consist of two syllables and two Latin word parts. Gaze upon a phalanx of a hundred of them:

abstract	convert	import	object	pervert
addict	convict	indent	offprint	present
address	decrease	incline	offset	proceeds
admit	defect	increase	overdraft	process
affect	digest	indent	overdraw	progress
combat	discard	implant	overdrive	project
combine	discharge	insert	overhang	protest
commune	disconnect	insult	overhaul	segment
compact	discount	intercept	overlap	survey
compound	discourse	interrupt	overlay	suspect
compress	dislike	intrigue	overload	torment
conduct	dismount	invite	overlook	transform
confines	dispatch	miscount	override	transplant
conflict	escort	misdeal	overrule	transport
conscript	excerpt	mishit	overrun	traverse
consort	exploit	mismatch	overstock	update
construct	export	misplay	overthrow	upgrade
consult	extract	misprint	overuse	uplift
contest	ferment	misquote	perfume	upload
contrast	impact	misuse	permit	upset

Adding icing to the pro-verbal cake, here are thirty *re-* words that also fit the trochaic (DA-dum)-iambic (da-DUM) noun-verb pattern:

rebel	record	rehash	repeat	reset
rebound	recount	reject	replay	retake
rebuy	redo	relapse	reprint	retard
recall	refill	relay	reraise	revote
recap	refund	reload	rerun	rewind
recoil	refuse	remake	research	rewrite

In some three-syllable words, the stress shifts from the front of the noun to the middle, but not the end, of the verb, as in *attribute, remodel,* and *influence,* while a number of adjective-verb and adjective-noun switches evince a shift of stress and/or a change in vowel sound, as in *–ate* words such as *approximate, articulate, deliberate, elaborate, incarnate, intimate,* and *laminate,* as well as the likes of *absent, invalid, minute, perfect,* and *prevent.* Finally, if you speak

"Southernese," you probably can add examples to the above lists with the likes of the forestressed nouns POH-leece, CEE-ment, and DIS-play.

As the distinctions between one part of speech and another become blurred, it seems that almost any interchange is possible. This grammatical malleability of our English language can be captured in a four-by-four matrix:

	Noun	Adjective	Adverb	Verb
Noun	_____	head	home	face
Adjective	red	_____	well	Muddy
Adverb	outs	in	_____	Up
Verb	walks	transplant	roughshod	_____

1. Mary became the _head_ bookkeeper. (noun to adjective)

2. Let's go home. (noun to adverb)

3. We must face the problem. (noun to verb)

4. The business is in the red. (adjective to noun)

5. Jasper plays tennis well. (adjective to adverb; well came into the language as an adjective)

6. Did you muddy your dress? (adjective to verb)

7. Frank is on the outs with his boss. (adverb to noun)

8. He's the leader of the in-group. (adverb to adjective)

9. The poker players decided to up the stakes. (adverb to verb)

10. He takes long walks every day. (verb to noun)

11. She was saved by a successful transplant operation. (verb to adjective)

12. He rode roughshod over his employees. (verb to adverb; here shod, "shoed," a verb, becomes an adverb when compounded)

A number of other transmogrifications are possible beyond the Noun-Adjective-Adverb-Verb matrix:

13. Try Slime Shampoo for a lovelier you. (pronoun to noun)

14. I believe in gender equality, but please don't he or she me to death. (pronouns to verbs)

15. He's a real he-man. (pronoun to adjective)

16. Who is the next famous person that the press will out? (preposition to verb)

17. We must learn to do without. (preposition to adverb)

18. Don't give me any ifs, ands, or buts. (conjunctions to nouns)

19. But me no buts. (conjunction to verb)

20. The crowd oohed and ahhed. (interjections to verbs)

COMPOUNDS
COMPOUNDED

THE CHALLENGE:

Just how grammatically versatile
are compound words?

Since earliest times, speakers of English, true to the Germanic roots of their language, have created thousands of new words by joining together two (or more) independent morphemes (meaning-bearing elements) to form compound words. Compounds are amazingly versatile creatures that can be employed in any grammatical function: an a noun (*earthquake*), as a pronoun (*herself*), as an adjective *(colorblind)*, as an adverb (*underground*), as a verb (*overachieve*), as a preposition (*without*), or as a conjunction (*whenever*).

Have a look at this four-by-four matrix featuring the four major parts of speech—noun, verb, adjective, and adverb. All sixteen possibilities for combination repose therein:

	Noun	Adjective	Adverb	Verb
Noun	bookcase	homesick	flashback	godsend
Adjective	madman	bittersweet	blackout	freeload
Adverb	upshot	evergreen	henceforth	underplay
Verb	scarecrow	fail-safe	diehard	hearsay

Independent word elements may unite in such ingenious ways that the part of speech of a compound may be different from that of either of its components, as in the last two entries above: *die* (verb) + *hard* (adverb) = *diehard* (noun); *hear* (verb) + *say* (verb) = *hearsay* (noun or adjective). This protean aspect of compounds raises the question: can the third dimension of the above matrix be filled out so that each of the sixteen types function as a noun, adjective, adverb, and verb, yielding a total of sixty-four entries?

Here, in a four-by-four-by-four matrix, is my response to that burning question that surely every speaker of English has been asking. In the matrix that follows, I avoid resorting to grammatical suffixes, such as *–ly.*

	Noun- Noun	Noun- Adjective	Noun- Adverb	Noun- Verb
Noun	bookcase	bootblack	flashback	godsend
Adjective	shipshape	homesick	head-on	handmade
Adverb	sidesaddle	knee-deep	hands down	shell-shocked
Verb	tiptoe	court-martial	zero in	Handpick

	Adjective-Noun	Adjective-Adjective	Adjective-Adverb	Adjective-Verb
Noun	madman	deaf-mute	blackout	slowpoke
Adjective	commonplace	bittersweet	straightforward	rough-hewn
Adverb	barefoot	northeast	moreover	roughshod
Verb	blackball	high-low	black in	Freeload

	Adverb-Noun	Adverb-Adjective	Adverb-Adverb	Adverb-Verb
Noun	upshot	evergreen	whereabouts	downpour
Adjective	offhand	overdue	never-never	income
Adverb	overboard	outright	henceforth	overmatched
Verb	outlaw	outsmart	fast-forward	underplay

	Verb-Noun	Verb-Adjective	Verb-Adverb	Verb-Verb
Noun	scarecrow	speakeasy	diehard	hearsay
Adjective	breakneck	fail-safe	tumbledown	slapdash
Adverb	makeshift	punch-drunk	worn out	straddle mount
Verb	pickpocket	blow-dry	give up	make believe

I lovingly labored on this verbal Rubik's Cube for about thirty hours over the course of two days, and the last three compounds I was finally able to insert were *high-low, blow-dry*, and *fast-forward*, all recent but solidly entrenched compounds in English. One who leads out first a high card and then a low card in bridge *high-lows*. Two football linemen who block a defensive player high and low are *high-lowing*. One who blows her or his hair dry *blow-dries* it. And one who presses the appropriate button on a tape recorder or video unit *fast-forwards*.

The shiny newness of the compounds *high-low, blow-dry*, and *fast-forward* (just about the only examples I could conjure up for their respective niches) indicates the experimental vigor of modern English. Somehow there has grown up over time a collective unconscious among English speakers, who, it seems, would not be satisfied until the language evolved to the point where all sixty-four rooms in the matrix could be occupied. What bound us together to join in fearful, functional symmetry the myriad components of that monumental cube? Was our achievement mere coincidence and blind luck, or was it somehow programmed into the microchips of our brains?

Most of the above entries are self-explanatory, but some require a brief exegesis. *Shell-shocked, overmatched, worn out,* and *punch-drunk* act adverbially in sentences such as "He left the ring shell-shocked, overmatched, worn out, and punch-drunk."

I do not pretend that the matrices above cover all possible grammatical alliances for compounds. Additional combinations include *he-man* (pronoun + noun = noun), *himself* (pronoun + noun = pronoun), *whoever* (pronoun + adverb = pronoun), *each other* (adjective + noun = pronoun), *into* (adverb + adverb = preposition), *undercut* (preposition + verb = verb), *within* (preposition + preposition = preposition), and *whenever* (adverb + adverb = conjunction).

A COMPOUND
SUBJECT

READER CHALLENGE:

To compound your knowledge of compound words, try your hand and mind at the triple-play game that follows. For the first section, examine the three words in each list and think of a word that could come before each of the three to form a compound, as in *black* bird board smith.

1. hunter, line, quarters 2. board, note, ring 3. grenade, out, writing 4. line, pass, product 5. country, roads, word

6. lands, school, way 7. ball, locker, print 8. book, key, port 9. hat, liner, nosed 10. hog, map, race

11. cut, net, line 12. bank, brother, feud 13. bread, change, hand 14. draw, hold, stand 15. bow, check, drop

16. boat, letter, seat 17. run, stretch, town 18. card, lift, mask 19. breaker, mill, shear 20. job, plow, shoe

Now consider the three words in each of the following lists and think of a word that could come *after* each one to form a compound, as in back, first, short *hand*.

21. bank, cook, text 22. bull's, evil, private 23. curtain, lightning, ram 24. board, cake, side 25. high, lime, moon

26. back, fore, under 27. left, pop, turn 28. every, no, some 29. base, foot, odd 30. love, steam, tug

31. back, eye, whip 32. hoe, show, touch 33. back, over, sounding 34. by, cross, pass 35. by, over, under

36. hind, in, over 37. down, water, wind 38. magic, no, talk 39. hand, machine shot 40. big, hot, pot

Finally, supply the word that completes the compound begun by the first word and starts the compound completed by the second word, as in gentle *man* hole.

41. foot _____ point 42. front _____ backer 43. cook _____ case 44. space _____ shape 45. skeleton _____ note

46. tooth _____ ax 47. cow _____ scout 48. sweet _____ brush 49. open _____ tight 50. red _____ dog

Answers

1. head 2. key 3. hand 4. by 5. cross 6. high 7. foot 8. pass 9. hard 10. road

11. hair 12. blood 13. short 14. with 15. rain 16. love 17. home 18. face 19. wind 20. snow

21. book 22. eye 23. rod 24. walk 25. light 26. ground 27. over 28. one or body 29. ball 30. boat

31. lash 32. down 33. board 34. word 35. pass or play 36. sight 37. fall 38. show 39. gun 40. shot

41. ball 42. line 43. book 44. ship 45. key 46. pick 47. boy or girl 48. tooth 49. air 50. hot

HEADS WITHOUT TAILS

THE CHALLENGE:

How many negatives lack
positives, and how many plurals
are bereft of singulars?

When a pig gets laryngitis, is it then disgruntled?

But seriously . . .

What do you make of the fact that we can talk about certain things and ideas only when they are absent? Once they appear, our confounding English language doesn't allow us to describe them. Have you ever run into someone who was gruntled, combobulated, couth, sheveled, chalant, plussed, ruly, gainly, maculate, kempt, pecunious, peccable, assuming, or souciant?

Dubitably, evitably, controvertibly, and advertently, English is a choate, corrigible, defatiguable, delible, describable, dolent, imicable, scrutible, tractable, sensical language populated by a lot of heads without tails and odds without ends. These words and expressions are like single socks nestled in a drawer; they never become part of a pair.

In his poem "Gloss," David McCord spoofs the ability of the English language to engender negatives but not the corresponding positives:

> I know a little man both ept and ert.
> An intro-? Extro-? No, he's just a vert.
> Sheveled and couth and kempt, pecunious, ane,
> His image trudes upon the ceptive brain.
>
> When life turns sipid and the mind is traught,
> The spirit soars as I would sist it ought.
> Chalantly then, like any gainly goof,
> My digent self is sertive, choate, loof.

Have you ever seen a horseful carriage or a strapful gown? Have you ever heard a promptu speech? Have you ever met a sung hero or a repressible, corrigible punster, or trepid coward? I know people who are no slouch, but I've never actually met a slouch. I know people who are no spring chickens, but where, pray tell, are the people who *are* spring chickens? Where are the people who actually *would* hurt a fly? All the time I meet people who *are* great shakes, who actually *did* squat, who *can* cut the mustard, who *can* fight City Hall, who *are* my cup of tea, who *would* lift a finger to help, who *do* have a mean bone in their body, who *would* give you the time of day, who find that life *is* a bed of roses, who *can* make heads or tails of something, who actually *have* experienced requited love, who actually *are* playing with a full deck, and whom I *would* touch with a ten-foot pole, but I can't talk about them in English—and that *is* a laughing matter.

These negatives that lack corresponding positives have been labeled "unnegatives," and they are close kin to "unplurals"—plurals that don't possess corresponding singulars. Like *gruntled, sheveled,* and *combobulated,* we behold another category of heads without tails.

Doesn't it seem just a little wifty that we can make amends but never just one amend and that no matter how carefully we comb through the annals of history, we can never explore just one annal? Why can't a moderately messy room be in a shamble? Why can't a moderately depressed person be out of a sort, a moderately indebted person be in an arrear, and moderately conspiratorial people be in a cahoot?

Why is it that we can never pull a shenanigan, read a funny, sing a blue, consume an egg Benedict, be in a doldrum, suffer from a mump, a measle, a ricket, or a shingle or experience just one jitter, willy, delirium tremen, or heebie-jeebie? Why, sifting through the wreckage of a room blown to smithereens, can we never find just one smithereen?

Indeed, this whole business of plurals that don't have matching singulars reminds me to ask this burning question, one that has flummoxed scholars for centuries: If you have a bunch of odds and ends and you get rid of or sell off all but one of them, what do you call that single item you're left with?

FOXEN IN
THE HENHICE

THE CHALLENGE:

How many wacky plural nouns
can be crammed
into a single interview?

R ecently I undertook an extensive study of American dialects, and a friend told me about a farmer named Eben Pluribus who spoke a most unusual kind of English. So I went to visit Farmer Pluribus, and here is a transcript of our interview:

"Mr. Pluribus, I hear that you've had some trouble on the farm."

"Well, young fella, times were hard for a spell. Almost every night them danged foxen were raiding my henhice."

"Excuse me, sir," I interjected. "Don't you mean *foxes*?"

"Nope, I don't," Pluribus replied. "I use oxen to plow my fields, so it's foxen that I'm trying to get rid of."

"I see. But what are *henhice*?" I asked.

"Easy. One mouse, two mice; one henhouse, two henhice. You must be one of them city slickers, but surely you know that henhice are what them birds live in that, when they're little critters, they utter all them peep."

"I think I'm beginning to understand you, Mr. Pluribus. But don't you mean *peeps*?"

"Nope, I mean *peep*. More than one sheep is a flock of sheep, and more than one peep is a bunch of peep. What do you think I am, one of them old ceet?"

"I haven't meant to insult you, sir," I gulped. "But I can't quite make out what you're saying."

"Then you must be a touch slow in the head," Farmer Pluribus shot back. "One foot, two feet; one coot, two ceet. I'm just trying to easify the English language, so I make all regular plural nouns irregular. Once they're all irregular, then it's just the same like they're all regular."

"Makes perfect sense to me," I mumbled.

"Good boy," said Pluribus, and a gleam came into his eyes. "Now, as I was trying to explain, them pesky foxen made such a fuss that all the meese and lynges have gone north."

"Aha!" I shouted. "You're talking about those big antlered animals, aren't you? One goose, two geese; one moose, a herd of meese. And *lynges* is truly elegant—one sphinx, a row of sphinges; one lynx, a litter of lynges."

"You're a smart fella, sonny," smiled Pluribus. "You see, I used to think that my cose might scare away them foxen, but the cose were too danged busy chasing rose."

"Oh, oh. You've lost me again," I lamented. "What are *cose* and *rose*?"

"Guess you ain't so smart after all," Pluribus sneered. "If *those* is the plural of *that*, then *cose* and *rose* got to be the plurals of *cat* and *rat*."

"Sorry that I'm so thick, but I'm really not one of those people who talk through their hose," I apologized, picking up Pluribus's cue. "Could you please tell me what happened to the foxen in your henhice?"

"I'd be deee-lighted to," answered Pluribus. "What happened was that my brave wife, Una, grabbed one of them frying pen and took off after them foxen."

I wondered for a moment what *frying pen* were and soon realized that because the plural of *man* is *men*, the plural of *pan* had to be *pen*.

"Well," Pluribus went right on talking, "the missus wasn't able to catch them foxen so she went back to the kitchen and began throwing dish and some freshly made pice at them critters."

That part of the story stumped me for a time, until I reasoned that a school of fish is made up of fish and more than one die make a roll of dice so that Una Pluribus must have grabbed a stack of dishes and pies.

Pluribus never stopped. "Them dish and pice sure scarified them foxen, and the pests have never come back. In fact, the rest of the village heard about what my wife did, and they were so proud that they sent the town band out to the farm to serenade her with tubae, harmonicae, accordia, fives, and dra."

"Hold up!" I gasped. "Give me a minute to figure out those musical instruments. The plural of *formula* is *formulae*, so the plurals of *tuba* and *harmonica* must be *tubae* and *harmonicae*. And the plurals of *phenomenon* and *criterion* are *phenomena* and *criteria*, so the plural of *accordion* must be *accordia*."

"You must be one of them genii," Pluribus exclaimed.

"Maybe," I blushed. "One cactus, two cacti; one alumnus, an association of alumni. So one genius, a seminar of genii. But let me get back to those instruments. The plurals of *life* and *wife* are *lives* and *wives*, so the plural of *fife* must be *fives*. And the plural of *medium* is *media*, so the plural of *drum* must be *dra*. Whew! That last one was tough."

"Good boy, sonny. Well, my wife done such a good job of chasing away them foxen that the town newspaper printed up a story and ran a couple of photographim of her holding them pen, dish, and pice."

My brain was now spinning in high gear, so it took me but an instant to realize that Farmer Pluribus had regularized one of the most exotic plurals in the English language—*seraph, seraphim*; so *photograph, photographim*. I could imagine all those Pluribi bathing in their bathtubim, as in *cherub, cherubim; bathtub, bathtubim*.

"Well," crowed Pluribus. "I was mighty pleased that everybody was so nice to the missus, but that ain't no surprise since folks in these here parts show a lot of respect for their methren."

"*Brother, brethren; mother, methren*," I rejoined. "That thought makes me want to cry. Have you any boxen of Kleenices here?"

"Sure do, young fella. And I'm tickled pink that you've caught on to the way I've easified the English language. One index, two indices, and one appendix, two appendices. So one Kleenex, two Kleenices. Makes things simpler, don't it?"

I was so grateful to Farmer Pluribus for having taught me his unique dialect that I took him out to one of them local cafeteriae. Then I reported my findings to the American Dialect Society by calling from one of the telephone beeth in the place.

Yep, you've got it. One tooth, two teeth. One telephone booth, two telephone beeth. Makes things simpler, don't it?

HIGHLY IRREGULAR
VERBS

THE CHALLENGE:

How many illusory sequences
can be constructed for strong,
irregular verbs?

Most English adjectives take on the suffixes *-er* and *-est* as they journey from their base forms to their comparative and superlative incarnations, as in *smart smarter smartest* and *funny funnier funniest*. Some intrepid logologists have created sequences of unrelated words that look like adjectival progressions but aren't.

The adventure of fabricating illusory sequences of adjectives is fraught with near misses (which are, of course, really "near hits"). *Pry-prior-priest* and *mole-molar-molest* come so close, except that their comparative forms lack the crucial *-er* suffix. *Should-shoulder* promise much, but *shouldest* doesn't deliver as a superlative. *Deter-detest* and *infer-infest* are jazzy comparatives and superlatives, but *det* and *inf* don't work as base words.

Still, we may capture four clever impostors:

bee	beer	beest
hon	honer	honest
p	per	pest
temp	temper	tempest

Triads of irregular verbs lend themselves much more generatively to the letter play of illusory patterns.

English verbs fall into two great classes: regular and irregular. Most verbs are regular, forming their past and present perfect tenses by adding *-d, -ed,* or *-t,* as in *I walk. I walked. I have walked. I bend. I bent. I have bent.* Irregular verbs, in contrast, go back in time through internal vowel changes, as in *begin* (present tense) *began* (past tense) *begun* (present perfect tense), *sing sang sung, see saw seen,* and *write wrote written.* Note that, in strong, irregular verbs like *ring rang rung* the vowels move from the front of your mouth to the back of your throat as the verbs retreat in time. These verbs are labeled irregular because they exhibit seventeen different patterns, from the unchanging *I set, I set, I set* to the kaleidoscopic *I am, I was, I have been.*

Tense Times with Verbs

The verbs in English are a fright.
How can we learn to read and write?
Today we speak, but first we spoke;
Some faucets leak, but never loke.
Today we write, but first we wrote;
We bite our tongues, but never bote.

Each day I teach, for years I've taught,
And preachers preach, but never praught.
This tale I tell; this tale I told;
I smell the flowers, but never smold.

If knights still slay, as once they slew,
Then do we play, as once we plew?
If I still do as once I did,
Then do cows moo, as they once mid?

I love to win, and games I've won;
I seldom sin, and never son.
I hate to lose, and games I've lost;
I didn't choose, and never chost.

I love to sing, and songs I sang;
I fling a ball, but never flang.
I strike that ball, that ball I struck;
This poem I like, but never luck.

I take a break, a break I took;
I bake a cake, but never book.
I eat that cake, that cake I ate;
I beat an egg, but never bate.

I often swim, as I once swam;
I skim some milk, but never skam.
I fly a kite that I once flew;
I tie a knot, but never tew.

I see the truth, the truth I saw;
I flee from falsehood, never flaw.
I stand for truth, as I once stood;
I land a fish, but never lood.

About these verbs I sit and think.
These verbs don't fit. They seem to wink
At me, who sat for years and thought
Of verbs that never fat or wrought.

In my cobbling together of illusory patterns for irregular verbs, I have adhered to three rubrics:

(1) All three words in the illusory pattern must share the last letters of the original verbs. At the heart of logology is the accidence of letters, not the similarity of sound. In fact, *divergences* of sound are welcomed, as long as the last letters remain identical to the original model. Homophones are thus excluded, as in *rise-rose-risen / prize-prose-prison* and *take-took-taken / bake-book-bacon.* I felt that if homophony were allowed, the number of illusory patterns would expand uncontrollably and the integrity of the category would be breached.

(2) The illusory pattern must reflect a sequence of three different verb forms. Leaping off from triads of only two forms, such as *cling-clung-clung / ding-dung-dung* and *bring-brought-brought / sing-sought-sought*, is just too easy and drab. Single-form triads of the *cost-cost-cost* and *set-set-set* type are, of course, also barred.

(3) The triads may not include two or more verbs related to each other, such as *eat ate eaten / beat-bate-beaten* and *drive-drove-driven / strive-strove-striven.*

Like the hunt for illusory adjectives, the quest for highly irregular verbs is fraught with false starts: *fall-fell-fallen / ball-bell-_____* and *tread-trod-trodden / read-rod-_____* burst from the starting blocks but lack acceptable finishers. *Freeze-froze-frozen / _____-doze-dozen* and *strike-struck-stricken / _____-chuck-chicken* and *_____-suck-sicken* end spectacularly but lack corresponding base forms. *Begin-began-begun / shin-_____-shun* and *prove-proved-proven / cove-_____-coven* fall flat in the middle distance department.

But patience is richly rewarded in this enterprise. Take the most irregular of all English verbs—verbs of being. The singular *am, was been* yield *Pam, pas, peen*, while *are were been* spark forth *pare-pere-peen.*

Now the stage is set for the revelation of more than sixty additional highly irregular verbs (which often aren't verbs at all):

PRESENT	PAST	PRESENT PERFECT	PRESENT	PAST	PRESENT PERFECT
begin	began	begun	bin	ban	bun
			din	Dan	dun
			fin	fan	fun
			gin	gan	gun
			pin	pan	pun
			shin	Shan	shun
			tin	tan	tun
bite	bit	bitten	kite	kit	kitten
break	broke	broken	teak	toke	token
do	did	done	bo	bid	bone
			ho	hid	hone
			lo	lid	lone
			o	id	one
draw	drew	drawn	daw	dew	dawn
			paw	pew	pawn
			yaw	yew	yawn
drink	drank	drunk	dink	dank	dunk
			skink	skank	skunk
			think	thank	thunk
fly	flew	flown	cry	crew	crown
			dry	drew	drown
			my	mew	mown
			y	ew	own

PRESENT	PAST	PRESENT PERFECT	PRESENT	PAST	PRESENT PERFECT
go	went	gone	bo	bent	bone
			do	dent	done
			ho	hent	hone
			lo	lent	lone
			po	went	pone
			so	sent	sone
			to	tent	tone
grow	grew	grown	brow	brew	brown
			crow	crew	crown
			dow	dew	down
			ow	ew	own
lie	lay	lain	Brie	bray	brain
			fie	fay	fain
			pie	pay	pain
			vie	vay	vain
ring	rang	rung	bing	bang	bung
			ding	dang	dung
			ping	pang	pung
			ting	tang	tung
see	saw	seen	pee	paw	peen
			tee	taw	Teen

PRESENT	PAST	PRESENT PERFECT	PRESENT	PAST	PRESENT PERFECT
slay	*slew*	*slain*	bray	brew	brain
(the most generative triad)			dray	drew	drain
			fay	few	fain
			gray	grew	grain
			jay	Jew	Jain
			may	mew	main
			nay	new	Nain
			pay	pew	pain
			say	sew	sain
			spay	spew	Spain
			stay	stew	stain
			stray	strew	strain
swim	*swam*	*swum*	dim	dam	dum
			him	ham	hum
			rim	ram	rum
			scrim	scram	scrum
			slim	slam	slum
tear	*tore*	*torn*	bear	bore	born
			Lear	lore	lorn
			pear	pore	porn
wake	*woke*	*woken*	take	toke	token
write	*wrote*	*written*	mite	mote	mitten

READER CHALLENGE:

Here are a dozen trouble-making
verbs that become nettlesome
as they go back in time. Identify
the past-tense form (or forms)
of each verb:

1. dive   4. kneel   7. shine   10. tread

2. fly   5. light   8. sneak   11. wake

3. hang   6. plead   9. swim   12. weave

Answers

1. *Dived. Dove* is acceptable but less common. 2, *Flew*, unless you're describing what a player did when he hit a ball high in the air and *flied out.* 3. Pictures, coats, and holiday ornaments are *hung*, but criminals found guilty of capital offenses are *hanged*, or at least they used to be. 4. *Kneeled* or *knelt*, but *knelt* is way more common, as are the similarly sounded *dream-dreamt* and *leap-leapt.*

5. *Lighted* and *lit* are equally acceptable. 6. *Pleaded*, rather than *pled*, is the strongly preferred past and present-perfect tense form, including "pleaded guilty." 7. *Shone*, if the verb means "to radiate," *shine*, if the verb means "to polish," "While the sun shone, he shined his best pair of shoes." 8. *Sneaked* is the more prevalent and acceptable form.

9. As in *shrink-shrank-shrunk* and *spring-sprang-sprung, swam* is the preferable past-tense form of *swim.* 10. *Trod* is preferable to *treaded* as a past-tense form of *tread*, except when one is swimming, as in "She treaded water." 11. *Wake* and its close kin *awake* are two verbs still in ferment with several possible past-tense forms. Nonetheless, *woke* and *awoke* are preferred. 12. *Wove* for making cloth, *weaved* for moving in a zigzag pattern, although *wove* is also acceptable in that im-material context.

BUILDING A
SUPERSENTENCE

THE CHALLENGE:

What is the shortest sentence
one can construct that includes
all four grammatical phrases
and all three clauses?

I have long been convinced that the study of grammar need not
be an arcane, hermetically sealed exercise. Each year at St. Paul's
School, in Concord, New Hampshire, where I taught for almost
three decades, my students and I explored the structure of English,
from the parts of speech to phrases and clauses, applying our knowledge to usage, punctuation, and sentence creation.

"Every self-respecting mechanic," said John Dewey, "will call
the parts of an automobile by their right names because that is the

way to distinguish them." Thus it is with the writer. If Alexander Pope is correct in asserting that "true ease in writing comes from art, not chance," a naming of the grammatical parts will reduce the chance and enhance the art, even if those names are one day forgotten.

Ultimately, though, I believe that, in the words of structuralist Paul Roberts, "The best reason for studying grammar is that grammar is interesting." Grammar may not be glamorous in any glittery, Hollywood sense, but grammar can indeed be very interesting, even enchanting.

That enchantment can even include having fun—yes, fun!—with grammar and usage. Take the study of subject-verb combinations that we term clauses. What do you call a clause that comes every Christmas? A re-noun clause named Santa Clause. What do you call Santa Clause's wife? A relative clause. What do you call his elves? Subordinate clauses.

After my St. Paul's School scholars completed their study of descriptive English grammar, I often assigned them the writing of a "supersentence"—a single sentence containing one example of each of the four phrases and three subordinate clauses that are identified in English grammar. These are: prepositional phrase, participial phrase, gerund phrase, and infinitive phrase and adverb clause, adjective clause, and noun clause. These units may occur in any order in the assigned sentence.

One afternoon, while grading a batch of supersentences, I decided to try writing one myself, using the fewest words possible. (If you, dear reader, are a grammar jock, I invite you to try this feat before reading this narrative any further.) An hour of intense industry produced the following:

[1]*When people* [2]*who swing want* [3]*to see* [4]*what's happening, they try* [5]*attending parties* [6]*given* [7]*by hipsters.* (sixteen words)

The numbers indicate the beginning of each phrase and subordinate clause—(1) adverb clause: *When people who swing want to see what's happening* modifies the verb *try* in the main clause; (2) adjective clause: *who swing* modifies the noun *people*; (3) infinitive phrase: *to see what's happening* acts as the direct object of the verb *want*; (4) noun clause: *what's happening* acts as the object of the infinitive *to see*; (5) gerund phrase: *attending parties given by hipsters* acts as the direct object of the verb *try*; (6) participial phrase: *given by hipsters* modifies the noun *parties*; (7) prepositional phrase: *by hipsters* modifies the passive participial *given*. In subsequent sentences I shall provide numbers but leave the reader to identify the structures, which will appear in varying orders, so as to avoid cluttering these pages with labyrinthine explanations like this one.

I proudly presented my sixteen-word concoction to my departmental colleagues and to my students, who saw and were amazed. A few days later, I was summoned by an emissary from another tenth-grade English class that met a few rooms down the hall from my section, and there on the chalkboard was inscribed:

Fred, ¹*wanting* ²*to win* ³*by* ⁴*playing hard, practiced more* ⁵*than I,* ⁶*who knew* ⁷*he stank.* (fifteen words)

Among the triumphantly glowing faces in that alien classroom was that of Bruce Monrad, the finest young linguist in our school at that time. Bruce, it turned out, was the author of the fifteen-word supersentence, a creation that contains not only an elliptical adverb clause of comparison, *than I* [*practiced*], and a hidden noun clause, [*that*] *he stank,* but compacts the four phrases into the subordinate part of the sentence and the three clauses into the main part.

Not to be outdone, I labored mightily for the next few days and came up with:

¹*Stung* ²*by* ³*what happened, Lederer began* ⁴*trying* ⁵*to write better* ⁶*than Monrad,* ⁷*who fainted.* (fourteen words)

The next morning, I marched into the rival classroom and confidently wrote my new sentence on the blackboard, only to be instantly one-upped by young Monrad, who stepped forward and inscribed:

¹*Helping* ²*win* ³*by* ⁴*scoring more* ⁵*than I,* ⁶*who thought* ⁷*he stank, Fred overcame.* (thirteen words)

Here Bruce's brilliant excision of one word is accomplished in his second phrase, the infinitive, in which he lifts out the *to: Helping [to] win by scoring. . . .*

Now I was growing desperate. Word of the contest had spread throughout the school community. How could I ever again face my colleagues and my students if I were to be defeated by a mere strip-ling? The whole affair was beginning to give lie to William Cobbett's crabbed pronouncement: "The study of grammar is dry. It engages not the passions." Resolving not to give up, in, or out, I closeted my-self for the entire weekend. Finally, "Eureka!" flew from my lips as I emerged with this compacted supersentence:

¹*Helping* ²*win* ³*by* ⁴*overcoming* ⁵*what threatened, Lederer,* ⁶*who per-sisted* ⁷*when challenged, triumphed.* (twelve words)

In addition to being eminently readable, my fabrication is char-acterized by two clever strokes: a clause within a phrase within a phrase within a phrase within a phrase in the first five words, and the distillation of the adverb clause into a two-word cluster, *when [he was] challenged,* one word shorter than its predecessor, *more than I.* Not only are all the structures as concise as they can possibly be, but, with the exception of the subject, *Lederer,* all nouns, adjectives, and adverbs are now replaced by phrases and clauses. O frabjous day! Callooh! Callay!, I chortled in my joy. This sentence was traveling at the speed of light. It could become no smaller. Or so I thought.

On Monday morning, I strutted into Bruce's classroom and hu-bristically engraved my "ultimate" concatenation on the enemy's board, delivering a learned lecture proving that we had reached the end of the road supersentencewise. As I wheeled to leave, Bruce giggled, "Not so fast, Mr. Lederer." He explained that he too had dis-covered the formula for the two-word adverb clause and that, more-over, he had been able to replace *all* nouns, adjectives, and adverbs with phrases and clauses. He then chalked up:

¹*Whoever rebels,* ²*daring* ³*oppose* ⁴*by* ⁵*fighting* ⁶*when opposed,* ⁷*which overcomes, conquers.* (eleven words!)

While reaching the theoretical limit for supersentences, Bruce's creation is rather clunky, with the adjective clause *which overcomes* flapping loosely as a dangling modifier. Still, I have never been able to improve on the lad's effort, and I invite readers to submit more graceful and coherent supersentences of eleven words.

Like two kids choosing sides for a baseball game, Bruce and I ran our hands up the bat until there wasn't any wood left. Actually, though, we both won because when the game of grammar is played with a sense of humor and enjoyment, everyone can be a winner.

GLOSSARY

Anagrams – two or more words that contain exactly the same letters but in a different order. *Richard Lederer* is your *Riddler Reacher*. In a looping anagram, one letter travels from the front to the back or the back to the front of a word, as in *emanate-manatee.*

Anatonym – the name of a part of the body that can be made into a verb, as in "to face the music" and "to foot the bill."

Charading – breaking up a longer word into shorter words, as in *a caravan* is *a car, a van* and a *generation* is a *gene ration.* When it comes to paying taxes, so much of our money is *theirs* because they are *the IRS.*

Closed styling – the writing of two or more words with no space separating them, as in *highway.* In open styling a space or spaces separate the words, as in *high school.*

Compound – two or more independent morphemes (meaning-bearing elements) that are inseparably joined, often by closed styling and/or forestress. We can talk or write about a "dumb, clumsy waiter," but we cannot interpose a word between the elements in *dumbwaiter.*

Conversion (also called **function shift**) – Rail-jumping a word from one part of speech to another, as in the new verbs *text* and *friend.*

Eye rhymes – words that look like rhymes but don't sound like rhymes, as in "A *foul ghoul soul* loves *good blood food.*"

Grapheme – a unit, such as a letter or letter combination, in a writing system that represents a phoneme.

Heteronyms – words that look the same but don't sound the same and have different meanings: "The bandage was *wound* around the *wound*."

Homophones – words that sound the same but don't look the same and have different meanings: A naked grizzly is a *bare bear* and a pony with a sore throat a *hoarse horse.*

Inflexion – a change in form of a word, especially a pronoun, to indicate a change in function. In "The man sees the woman" and "The woman sees the man," the nouns *man* and *woman* change function from the first to the second sentence, but they don't change form. In "He sees her" and "She sees him," the two pronouns are inflected because they change form from the first to the second sentence to indicate function.

Irregular verb – a verb like *ring-rang-rung* that, as it goes back in time to past and present perfect, does not conform to the *walk-walked-walked* pattern of weak, regular verbs. Such verbs are irregular because they come in seventeen different patterns.

Isogram – a word, such as *ambidextrously* and *uncopyrightable,* in which no letter is repeated. The longer the better.

Kangaroo word – a larger word that contains, with letters in order, a smaller synonym of itself (called a joey). For example, *rambunctious* contains within its boundaries the synonymous joey *raucous.*

Linguistics – the scientific study of language, the various elements of the activity that most distinguishes human beings from the other animals who live on our planet.

Logology – the study of letter patterns in words, for example the fact that the word *facetious* parades the major vowels—*a, e, i, o,* and *u*—in alphabetical order and that the word *sequoia* is the shortest common word to house those vowels in any order.

Morpheme – a unit of meaning often smaller than a word. The sentence "The cats softly walked into our bedroom" consists of seven words and twelve morphemes:

words	1	2	3	4	5	6	7
	The	cats	softly	walked	into	our	bedroom.
morphemes	1	2 3	4 5	6 7	8 9	10	11 12

The, cat, soft, walk, in, to, our, bed, and *room* are independent morphemes that can stand alone as words. At the same time, *-s, -ly,* and *-ed* are bound morphemes that can't stand alone but that still possess meaning: "many," "in a manner," and "past tense."

Palindrome – a word (such as, in order of length, *mom, toot, level, redder, rotator,* and *redivider*), compound (*race car*), phrase (*a Santa at NASA*), sentence (*Sit on a potato pan, Otis*), or sentences (*Doc, note. I dissent. A fast never prevents a fatness. I diet on cod*) that read the same forward and backward.

Particle verb – a construction that looks like a verb modified by a prepositional phrase but isn't. In "I looked up the chimney," *up the chimney* is a prepositional phrase that modifies *looked*. But in "I looked up the word," *up* is part of the verb *look up*, meaning "to search for." One proof of the difference is that "Up the chimney I looked" is a comprehensible English sentence, while "Up the word I looked" is not.

Phoneme – the smallest unit of speech that can distinguish one word from another. In "The Cat in the Hat," the sounds represented by *c* and *h* are phonemes because they generate new meanings in *cat* and *hat*.

Univocalic – a long word that contains a single vowel used repeatedly, like *abracadabra*.

Word – a group of sounds or combination of letters to which people give meaning. Words are the smallest unit of meaning capable of independent use.

INDEX